Editor
Erica N. Russikoff, M.A.

Contributing Editor
Michael H. Levin, M.A., N.B.C.T.

Illustrators
Mark Mason
Renée Christine Yates

Cover Artist
Tony Carrillo

Editor in Chief
Ina Massler Levin, M.A.

Creative Director
Karen J. Goldfluss, M.S. Ed.

Imaging
Rosa C. See

Publisher

Mary D. Smith, M.S. Ed.

Teacher Created Resources, Inc.
6421 Industry Way
Westminster, CA 92683
www.teachercreated.com

ISBN: 978-1-4206-8844-3

©2010 Teacher Created Resources, Inc.
Reprinted, 2012 (PO5355)

Made in U.S.A.

Table of Contents

Table of Contents *(cont.)*

A Message From the
National Summer Learning Association

Dear Parents,

Did you know that all young people experience learning losses when they don't engage in educational activities during the summer? That means some of what they've spent time learning over the preceding school year evaporates during the summer months. However, summer learning loss *is* something that you can help prevent. Summer is the perfect time for fun and engaging activities that can help children maintain and grow their academic skills. Here are just a few:

- Read with your child every day. Visit your local library together, and select books on subjects that interest your child.

- Ask your child's teacher for recommendations of books for summer reading. The Summer Reading List in this publication is a good start.

- Explore parks, nature preserves, museums, and cultural centers.

- Consider every day as a day full of teachable moments. Measuring in recipes and reviewing maps before a car trip are ways to learn or reinforce a skill. Use the Learning Experiences in the back of this book for more ideas.

- Each day, set goals to accomplish. For example, do five math problems or read a chapter in a book.

- Encourage your child to complete the activities in books, such as *Summertime Learning*, to help bridge the summer learning gap.

Our vision is for every child to be safe, healthy, and engaged in learning during the summer. Learn more at *www.summerlearning.org* and *www.summerlearningcampaign.org*.

Have a *memorable* summer!

Ron Fairchild
Chief Executive Officer
National Summer Learning Association

How to Use This Book

As a parent, you know that summertime is a time for fun and learning. So it is quite useful that fun and learning can go hand in hand when your child uses *Summertime Learning*.

There are many ways to use this book effectively with your child. We list three ideas on page 6. (See "Day by Day," "Pick and Choose," and "All of a Kind.") You may choose one way on one day, and, on another day, choose something else.

Book Organization

Summertime Learning is organized around an eight-week summer vacation period. For each weekday, there are two lessons. Each Monday through Thursday, there is a math lesson. Additionally, during the odd-numbered weeks, there is a reading lesson on Monday and Wednesday and a writing lesson on Tuesday and Thursday. During the even-numbered weeks, these lessons switch days. (Reading lessons are on Tuesday and Thursday, and writing lessons are on Monday and Wednesday.) Friday features two Friday Fun activities (one typically being a puzzle). The calendar looks like this:

Day	Week 1	Week 2	Week 3	Week 4	Week 5	Week 6	Week 7	Week 8
M	Math -------- Reading	Math -------- Writing	Math -------- Reading	Math -------- Writing	Math -------- Reading	Math -------- Writing	Math -------- Reading	Math -------- Writing
T	Math -------- Writing	Math -------- Reading	Math -------- Writing	Math -------- Reading	Math -------- Writing	Math -------- Reading	Math -------- Writing	Math -------- Reading
W	Math -------- Reading	Math -------- Writing	Math -------- Reading	Math -------- Writing	Math -------- Reading	Math -------- Writing	Math -------- Reading	Math -------- Writing
Th	Math -------- Writing	Math -------- Reading	Math -------- Writing	Math -------- Reading	Math -------- Writing	Math -------- Reading	Math -------- Writing	Math -------- Reading
F	Friday Fun -------- Friday Fun	Friday Fun -------- Friday Fun	Friday Fun -------- Friday Fun	Friday Fun -------- Friday Fun	Friday Fun -------- Friday Fun	Friday Fun -------- Friday Fun	Friday Fun -------- Friday Fun	Friday Fun -------- Friday Fun

How to Use This Book
(cont.)

Day by Day

You can have your child do the activities in order, beginning on the first Monday of summer vacation. He or she can complete the two lessons provided for each day. It does not matter if math, reading, or writing is completed first. The pages are designed so that each day of the week's lessons are back to back. The book is also perforated. This gives you the option of tearing the pages out for your child to work on. If you opt to have your child tear out the pages, you might want to store the completed pages in a special folder or three-ring binder that your child decorates.

Pick and Choose

You may find that you do not want to have your child work strictly in order. Feel free to pick and choose any combination of pages based on your child's needs and interests.

All of a Kind

Perhaps your child needs more help in one area than another. You may opt to have him or her work only on math, reading, or writing.

Keeping Track

A Reward Chart is included on page 10 of this book, so you and your child can keep track of the activities that have been completed. This page is designed to be used with the stickers provided. Once your child has finished a page, have him or her put a sticker on the castle. If you don't want to use stickers for this, have your child color in a circle each time an activity is completed.

The stickers can also be used on the individual pages. As your child finishes a page, let him or her place a sticker in the sun at the top of the page. If he or she asks where to begin the next day, simply have him or her start on the page after the last sticker.

There are enough stickers to use for both the Reward Chart and the sun on each page. Plus, there are extra stickers for your child to enjoy.

Standards and Skills

Each activity in *Summertime Learning* meets one or more of the following standards and skills*. The activities in this book are designed to help your child reinforce the skills learned during third grade, as well as introduce new skills that will be learned in fourth grade.

Language Arts Standards

- ✪ Uses the general skills and strategies of the writing process
- ✪ Uses the stylistic and rhetorical aspects of writing
- ✪ Uses grammatical and mechanical conventions in written composition
- ✪ Gathers and uses information for research purposes
- ✪ Uses the general skills and strategies of the reading process
- ✪ Uses reading skills and strategies to understand and interpret a variety of literary texts
- ✪ Uses reading skills and strategies to understand a variety of informational texts
- ✪ Uses listening and speaking strategies for different purposes
- ✪ Uses viewing skills and strategies to understand and interpret visual media
- ✪ Understands the characteristics and components of the media

Mathematics Standards

- ✪ Uses a variety of strategies in the problem-solving process
- ✪ Understands and applies basic and advanced properties of the concepts of numbers
- ✪ Uses basic and advanced procedures while performing the processes of computation
- ✪ Understands and applies basic and advanced properties of the concepts of measurement
- ✪ Understands and applies basic and advanced properties of the concepts of geometry
- ✪ Understands and applies basic and advanced concepts of statistics and data analysis
- ✪ Understands and applies basic and advanced concepts of probability
- ✪ Understands and applies basic and advanced properties of functions and algebra

Writing Skills

- ✪ Uses strategies to draft and revise written work
- ✪ Use strategies to edit and publish written work
- ✪ Uses strategies to write for a variety of purposes
- ✪ Writes expressive compositions
- ✪ Writes in response to literature
- ✪ Uses descriptive language that clarifies and enhances ideas

Standards and Skills
(cont.)

Writing Skills *(cont.)*

- ✿ Uses paragraph form in writing
- ✿ Uses a variety of sentence structures in writing
- ✿ Uses nouns in written compositions
- ✿ Uses verbs in written compositions
- ✿ Uses adjectives in written compositions
- ✿ Uses conventions of punctuation in written compositions

Reading Skills

- ✿ Establishes a purpose for reading
- ✿ Makes, confirms, and revises simple predictions about what will be found in a text
- ✿ Uses a variety of context clues to decode unknown words
- ✿ Understands level-appropriate reading vocabulary
- ✿ Understands the author's purpose or point of view
- ✿ Uses reading skills and strategies to understand a variety of literary passages and texts
- ✿ Knows the defining characteristics of a variety of literary forms and genres
- ✿ Understands the basic concept of plot
- ✿ Makes inferences or draws conclusions about a character's qualities and actions
- ✿ Understands the way in which language is used in literary texts
- ✿ Summarizes and paraphrases information in texts
- ✿ Uses prior knowledge and experience to understand and respond to new information
- ✿ Understands structural patterns or organization in informational texts
- ✿ Understands different messages conveyed through visual media

Mathematics Skills

- ✿ Represents problem situations in a variety of forms
- ✿ Understands that some ways of representing a problem are more helpful than others
- ✿ Understands equivalent forms of basic percents, fractions, and decimals
- ✿ Understands the basic meaning of place value
- ✿ Understands the relative magnitude and relationships among whole numbers, fractions, decimals, and mixed numbers
- ✿ Multiplies and divides whole numbers

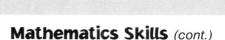

Mathematics Skills *(cont.)*

- ✿ Adds, subtracts, multiplies, and divides decimals

- ✿ Adds and subtracts simple fractions

- ✿ Uses specific strategies to estimate computations and to check the reasonableness of computational results

- ✿ Determines the effects of addition, subtraction, multiplication, and division on size and order of numbers

- ✿ Understands the properties of and the relationships among addition, subtraction, multiplication, and division

- ✿ Solves real-world problems involving number operations

- ✿ Knows the language of basic operations

- ✿ Knows the approximate size of basic standard units and the relationships between them

- ✿ Understands relationships between measures

- ✿ Understands basic properties of figures

- ✿ Predicts and verifies the effect of combining, subdividing, and changing basic shapes

- ✿ Uses motion geometry to understand geometric relationships

- ✿ Understands that data represent specific pieces of information about real-world objects or activities

- ✿ Organizes and displays data in simple bar graphs, pie charts, and line graphs

- ✿ Understands that data comes in many different forms and that collecting, organizing, and displaying data can be done in many ways

- ✿ Understands that when predictions are based on what is known about the past, one must assume that conditions stay the same from the past event to the predicted future event

- ✿ Uses basic sample spaces to describe and predict events

- ✿ Knows that a variable is a letter or symbol that stands for one or more numbers

- ✿ Solves simple open sentences involving operations on whole numbers

- ✿ Understands that numbers and the operations performed on them can be used to describe things in the real world and predict what might occur

* Standards and Skills used with permission from McREL (Copyright 2009, McREL. Midcontinent Research for Education and Learning. Address: 4601 DTC Boulevard, Suite 500, Denver, CO 80237. Telephone: 303-337-0990. Web site: www.mcrel.org/standards-benchmarks)

Reward Chart

Carnival Time

Directions: Solve each word problem. Show your work.

1. The carnival sold 1,542 adult passes; 4,791 senior passes; and 9,148 children's passes. How many passes were sold?

The carnival sold _____ passes.

2. There were 2,067 people waiting in line for the Ferris wheel. An hour later, 1,841 people were still waiting in line. How many people had their turn on the Ferris wheel?

_____ people had their turn.

3. The popcorn vendor sold 5,076 tubs of popcorn. 2,291 of the tubs of popcorn did not have any butter. How many tubs of popcorn did have butter?

_____ tubs of popcorn had butter.

4. At the snack bar, 5,027 servings of cotton candy; 2,386 bags of peanuts; and 1,081 snow cones were sold. How many snacks were sold in all?

_____ snacks were sold in all.

5. The Hot Dog Hut sold 7,356 hot dogs. 5,861 of the hot dogs were on sticks. How many hot dogs were not on sticks?

_____ hot dogs were not on sticks.

6. At the prize booth, the people were given 4,104 stuffed bears; 8,677 stuffed bunnies; and 3,437 stuffed pigs. How many prizes were given away in all?

_____ prizes were given away in all.

Rules of the Road

Directions: Find the meaning of each underlined word below. Using the definitions box below, put the letter of the answer on the blank line.

> a. absolutely necessary
> b. environment, area around you
> c. command, control
>
> d. tired, sleepy
> e. follow, do as others do

1. _____

2. _____

3. _____

4. _____

5. _____

"Listen up, people. Many of you are here because you have been caught breaking the rules of the road. That cannot be allowed. If you want to drive a car, it is very important that you ¹conform to certain rules and laws. You can't go too fast. You have to come to a complete stop at stop signs. It is ²essential that you are aware of your ³surroundings at all times. In order to ⁴helm a motor vehicle, you have to be awake and alert. You cannot be ⁵drowsy. You cannot be focused on other things. A car can be very dangerous if its driver is not paying attention."

Directions: On the blank line, write the best underlined word from above that expresses each idea.

6. I'm in charge of flying this plane.   _____

7. I'm ready for bed.   _____

8. I'm going to do what everyone else is doing.   _____

9. I must study if I want to get an "A" on the test.   _____

10. I live in a big city that has tall buildings. _____

Twists and Turns

Directions: An object can be rotated (or in other words—turned) clockwise by degrees. To what degree was each item turned? Circle the answer.

Examples:

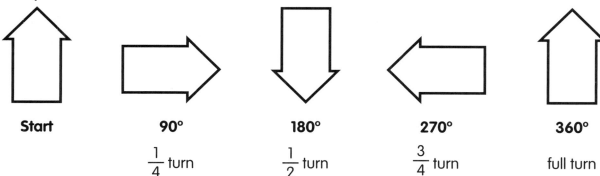

Start	90°	180°	270°	360°
	$\frac{1}{4}$ turn	$\frac{1}{2}$ turn	$\frac{3}{4}$ turn	full turn

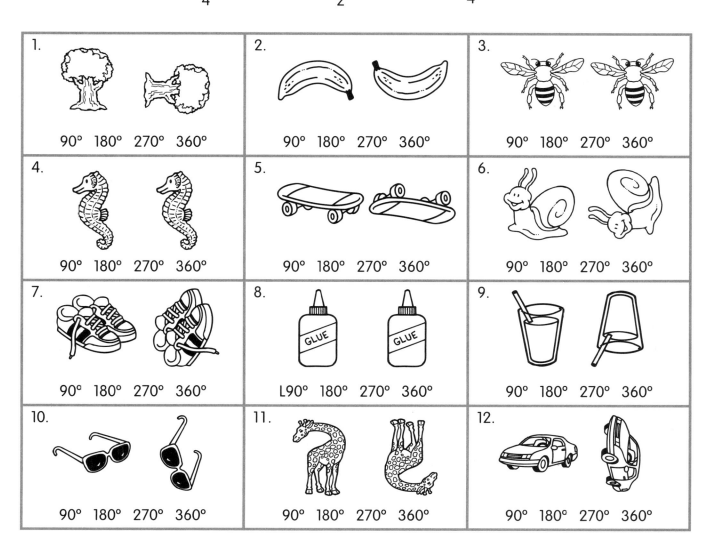

1. 90° 180° 270° 360°

2. 90° 180° 270° 360°

3. 90° 180° 270° 360°

4. 90° 180° 270° 360°

5. 90° 180° 270° 360°

6. 90° 180° 270° 360°

7. 90° 180° 270° 360°

8. L90° 180° 270° 360°

9. 90° 180° 270° 360°

10. 90° 180° 270° 360°

11. 90° 180° 270° 360°

12. 90° 180° 270° 360°

Cause and Effect

Directions: Complete the chart below. The left side of the chart is for the cause, and the right side of the chart is for the effect. Make sure that your answers make sense.

Cause	Effect
1. I tripped on the steps at school.	1. _____ _____ _____
2. _____ _____ _____	2. The dog was soaking wet!
3. I scored the winning goal in our soccer game.	3. _____ _____ _____
4. _____ _____ _____	4. My mom is very happy today.
5. I completed my homework.	5. _____ _____ _____

Draw the Bars

Directions: Using the information below, make a bar graph. Draw the bars to show how many hours a week these five children spend playing outside or watching television.

Name	Outside (Hours)	Television (Hours)
Barbara	8	12
Joe	6	20
Jennifer	14	10
Michael	20	6
Sandra	16	10

Use the colors in the key below to make your bar graph. The first one has been done for you.

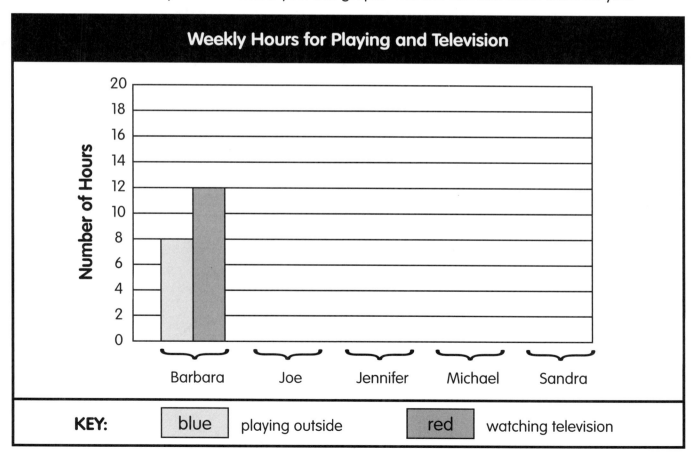

Tiger

Directions: Read the following paragraph. Then, identify the main idea, and write two supporting details. Write them in the graphic organizer below.

Tiger was the funniest cat we have ever had. He was the first cat to start drinking from our fish aquarium. I would laugh so hard every time I saw Tiger perched up on the fish aquarium, lapping up water from the water filter system! He never bothered the fish; he just loved to drink their water! Another funny thing that Tiger did was drink from the dog's bath water. Whenever we would be giving the dog a bath, Tiger would waltz over and start lapping up water from the tub. I don't think the dog appreciated that, but we sure thought it was funny! Tiger was definitely a very funny cat.

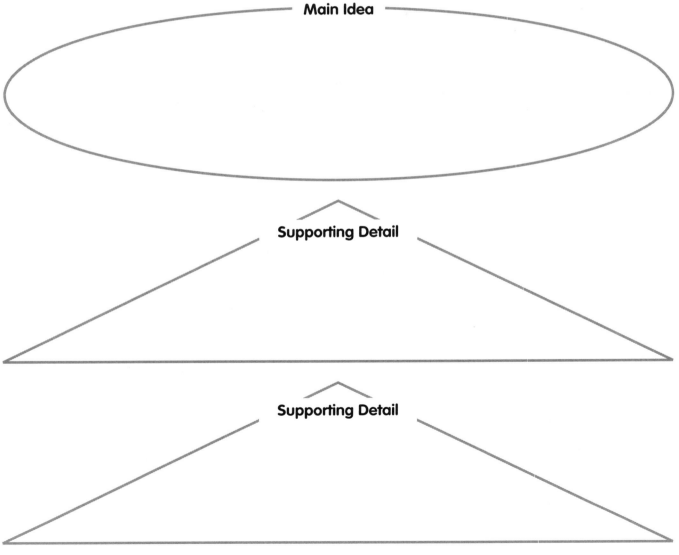

Main Idea

Supporting Detail

Supporting Detail

Food Fractions

Directions: Solve these fraction word problems.

Example: Three girls bought a double chocolate cake. Joanna ate $\frac{1}{4}$ of the cake. Michelle ate $\frac{3}{8}$ of the cake. How much was left for Sara?

   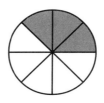   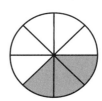

one whole cake

$= \frac{8}{8}$

Joanna ate $\frac{1}{4}$

$(\frac{2}{8} = \frac{1}{4})$

of the cake.

Michelle ate $\frac{3}{8}$
of the cake.

$\frac{3}{8}$ of the cake
was left for Sara.

1. Susan and Julie bought a ham and pineapple pizza. Susan ate $\frac{3}{7}$ of the pizza. How much was left for Julie? _____

2. Your best friend and you go to Pie Palace for pie. You eat $\frac{5}{6}$ of the pie. How much pie is left for your friend? _____

3. Your baseball coach bought a vanilla and strawberry cake to share with the team. The coach ate $\frac{7}{10}$ of the cake. How much cake was left for the team? _____

4. Your dad bought one whole vegetarian pizza from Pizza Paradise. Your sister ate $\frac{5}{8}$ of the pizza before you got home. How much pizza was left for you? _____

5. James and Ralph bought a pumpkin pie. James ate $\frac{2}{3}$ of the pie. How much pie was left for Ralph? _____

6. The third-grade teacher and the fourth-grade teacher bought a chocolate and raspberry cake. The fourth-grade teacher ate $\frac{7}{12}$ of the cake. How much cake was left for the third-grade teacher? _____

Silly Stories

Directions: Choose one of the following story starters, and write a silly story.

> ☼ **Story Starter #1:** Katie lay in bed staring at the water stain right over her head on the ceiling. It was shaped like a key, and she often imagined it was a map of a different country.
>
> ☼ **Story Starter #2:** "Look!" Jake pointed a finger at the light flickering through the trees beyond the cabin window. Colin didn't answer. Instead, he covered his head with his sleeping bag.
>
> ☼ **Story Starter #3:** Once upon a time, there was a princess who lived in a castle by the sea. She could not speak, but everyone enjoyed her sweet smile and kind deeds.
>
> ☼ **Story Starter #4:** Silently, I walked up to the edge of the crowd. The people were watching some activity in the middle of the courtyard. I stood on my toes and tried to see over the heads of those standing in front of me.

_____

_____

_____

_____

_____

Weekend Jokes

Directions: Choose a word from the Word Bank below to complete each joke. Each word is used once. When you finish, try out your jokes on a friend.

Word Bank

bring	hold	make	pay
enjoy	keep	move	want

1. Tourist: "How do you _____ your workers?"

   Rancher: "with buffalo bills"

2. What can you _____ in your left hand but never in your right hand?

   Answer: your right elbow

3. When can an old horse _____ as fast as a speeding train?

   Answer: when it's on the train

4. What can you put in a sandbag to _____ it weigh less?

   Answer: a hole

5. Why do ghosts _____ riding in elevators?

   Answer: It raises their spirits.

6. Which tool is the best to _____ to a gold rush?

   Answer: Take your pick.

7. Why do rabbits go on strike?

   Answer: They _____ a raise in celery.

8. How can you _____ your hair dry in the shower?

   Answer: Don't turn on the water.

Swimming Words

Directions: Read each word. Replace the first one or two letters to make a new word related to swimming.

1. teach: ____ ____ ____ ____ ____

2. boggles: ____ ____ ____ ____ ____ ____ ____

3. trim: ____ ____ ____ ____

4. link: ____ ____ ____ ____

5. save: ____ ____ ____ ____

6. tool: ____ ____ ____ ____

7. hand: ____ ____ ____ ____

8. five: ____ ____ ____ ____

9. face: ____ ____ ____ ____

10. pick: ____ ____ ____ ____

11. grip: ____ ____ ____ ____

12. cater: ____ ____ ____ ____ ____

13. skipper: ____ ____ ____ ____ ____ ____ ____

14. bloat: ____ ____ ____ ____ ____

15. taps: ____ ____ ____ ____

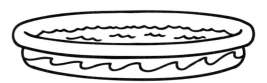

Operations

Directions: Read each problem. Then, circle or write your answers. Show your work on #1, 3, and 4.

1. Sarah is climbing a mountain that is 1,905 feet high. She has already climbed 489 feet. How many more feet does Sarah still need to climb in order to make it to the top?

   a. 2,394 ft.

   b. 1,584 ft.

   c. 1,416 ft.

   d. 584 ft.

2. Lee has 54 tools that he needs to separate into 6 piles. Which type of problem shown below would Lee use to find out how many tools need to be in each pile?

   a. $54 \times 6 =$ b. $54 \div 6 =$ c. $54 - 6 =$ d. $54 + 6 =$

3. Jennie has 160 stuffed bears in her collection. She is storing her collection of bears in containers that hold 20 stuffed bears. So far, she has already filled 5 containers. How many stuffed bears have NOT yet been put in a container for storage?

   _____

4. There were 76 birds on the playground at Dawson Elementary. Later, 58 birds flew away. Ten minutes later, another 19 joined the remaining birds. How many birds are now on the playground?

   _____

You're So Tense!

Verbs are an important part of sentences. Verbs may say what the subject does/did, or it may tell about the subject. Verbs can also tell us when something happens. If we want to change the time (tense) of a sentence, we need to change the form of the verb.

    Examples: Josie **wears** sunscreen. (present tense)

                     Josie **wore** sunscreen. (past tense)

                     Josie **will wear** sunscreen. (future tense)

Directions: These sentences are all written in different tenses. Name the tenses.

1. Yuki swims every day. _____ tense

2. This summer will be very hot. _____ tense

3. The sun burned the tips of my cat's ears. _____ tense

4. Jack builds sandcastles at the beach. _____ tense

5. I went to the beach last weekend. _____ tense

Directions: These sentences are all written in the present tense. Rewrite them in the past tense by changing their verbs.

6. Maria always wears a T-shirt over her bathing suit in the pool.

_____

_____

7. We pitch a tent for shade when we go on a picnic.

_____

_____

8. The day is hot and bright, so we wear hats and sunscreen.

_____

_____

Real World Math

Directions: Read each problem. Then, circle or write your answers on the lines. Show your work.

1. Howard made 3 flower beds in his backyard. They do not touch each other. Each flower bed was in the shape of an octagon. How many total sides were on all 3 flower beds?

_____

2. Wanda is making dough for kolaches that she is baking for a party. Wanda needs 2 tablespoons of salt for every 5 pounds of dough. Wanda is making 15 pounds of kolache dough. How many tablespoons of salt does she need?

   a. 2 tablespoons

   b. 4 tablespoons

   c. 6 tablespoons

   d. 10 tablespoons

3. When Jason left for work, the temperature was 32°F. By lunchtime, the temperature had risen 18 degrees. What was the temperature at lunchtime?

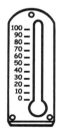

_____

4. Jim is putting holiday lights around the greenhouse in his yard. The greenhouse is in the shape of a rectangle that measures 6 feet wide and 8 feet long. How many feet of holiday lights will Jim need to complete this task?

8 ft.

6 ft.

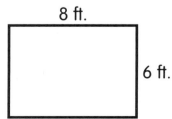

_____

Achoo!

Directions: Read the story, and then circle the correct answers below.

> "The recipe calls for two tablespoons of pepper," said Dillon.
>
> "Are you sure that's right?" asked Miranda. "I thought it was two teaspoons."
>
> "Yep, it's right. Remember, this is special soup to help Mom feel better."
>
> Miranda dumped the two tablespoons of pepper in and stirred the broth.
>
> Miranda sniffed the soup and began sneezing. "Whew! That's a lot of pepper."
>
> "It's going to be great," assured Dillon.
>
> The soup simmered for fifteen minutes. Dillon grabbed a soup bowl and began ladling the soup.
>
> "This is going to be so good for Mom's cold," said Miranda.
>
> Dillon dropped a cloth over his arm, and Miranda got out a tray.
>
> "Here we come, Mom," called Dillon.
>
> "Achoo!" said Mom. "What's this?"
>
> "It's homemade soup, just for you. It's going to work better than medicine."
>
> Mom took a big sniff of the soup in her lap and immediately started sneezing. She couldn't stop.
>
> "Oh, no! It has too much pepper!" exclaimed Miranda.
>
> "It's okay," interrupted Mom. "It's clearing my sinuses. How much pepper is in there?"
>
> "Two tablespoons," said Dillon.
>
> "I told you the recipe called for two **TEASPOONS!**" shouted Miranda.

1. Which of the following statements is *not* true?

    a. Miranda told Dillon to add two tablespoons of pepper.

    b. Mom was a good sport and made her kids feel good about helping her.

    c. Miranda was frustrated that there was too much pepper in the soup.

    d. Miranda trusted Dillon's instructions at the beginning of the passage.

2. What conclusions can be drawn about Miranda and Dillon's mom?

    a. She is an emotional person and cries a lot.   c. She will probably never eat soup again.

    b. She is supportive and understanding.   d. She tries to take over every situation.

3. After reading the passage, which of the following helps you answer the previous question?

    a. "How much pepper is in there?"   c. Mom took a big sniff of the soup.

    b. "It's okay . . . It's clearing my sinuses."   d. She couldn't stop sneezing.

Factor It Out

Directions: Fill in the missing factors. Use the multiplication chart on page 104 if you are unsure of your facts.

1. $9 \times \underline{\quad} = 54$

2. $3 \times \underline{\quad} = 36$

3. $10 \times \underline{\quad} = 60$

4. $8 \times \underline{\quad} = 64$

5. $\underline{\quad} \times 9 = 81$

6. $6 \times \underline{\quad} = 72$

7. $9 \times \underline{\quad} = 45$

8. $4 \times \underline{\quad} = 48$

9. $\underline{\quad} \times 7 = 42$

10. $\underline{\quad} \times 7 = 63$

11. $\underline{\quad} \times 9 = 63$

12. $5 \times \underline{\quad} = 55$

13. $6 \times \underline{\quad} = 36$

14. $\underline{\quad} \times 4 = 36$

15. $\underline{\quad} \times 6 = 54$

16. $\underline{\quad} \times 9 = 99$

17. $7 \times \underline{\quad} = 49$

18. $9 \times \underline{\quad} = 63$

19. $42 \div 7 = \underline{\quad}$

20. $54 \div 9 = \underline{\quad}$

21. $54 \div 6 = \underline{\quad}$

22. $12 \div 3 = \underline{\quad}$

23. $88 \div 8 = \underline{\quad}$

24. $48 \div 12 = \underline{\quad}$

Combine Them

One way to improve the quality of your paragraphs is to combine short, simple sentences.

Example: Jarrod was beside us. Jake was beside us. We did not know they were even in the house.

Jarrod and Jake were beside us before we knew they were even in the house.

Another way to make your sentences more interesting is to move around the parts of your sentences so they do not always start the same way—with the subject, for example.

Example: Before we knew they were even in the house, Jarrod and Jake were beside us.

Directions: Improve the sentences in the following paragraph by combining short, simple ones and by moving around the parts of the sentences so they do not always start the same way. (You may also change the order of the sentences and add or remove specific details.)

Trees Bear Gifts

Trees give us many things. Trees give us shade on hot days. Trees give us wood with which to build our homes. Trees give us fruit to eat. Trees give us leaves we can use for mulch. Trees provide shelter for the birds and other animals we enjoy. Trees give shelter from the rain. Trees can be good places to hide. Trees can be good places to play. Trees give us a place to build tree houses. Trees are also beautiful to look at. Trees may stay green all year long. Trees may lose all their leaves in the fall and winter. Trees may produce flowers.

How Much?

Directions: Use the prices to write addition problems. Find the sums.

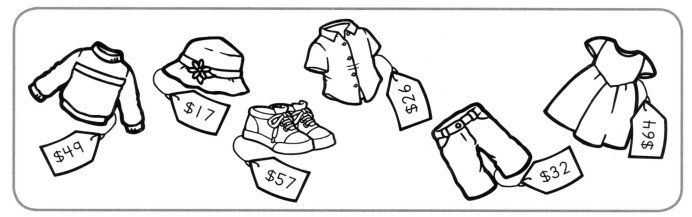

$49 $17 $57 $26 $32 $64

1.

_____ + _____ = _____

2.

_____ + _____ = _____

3.

_____ + _____ = _____

4.

_____ + _____ + _____ = _____

5.

_____ + _____ = _____

6.

_____ + _____ + _____ = _____

A True Athlete

Directions: Read the following story, and then number the events in the order in which they occurred.

Eddie has always been into sports. Before playing basketball, he played soccer. His soccer team went to the state championships and won a trophy when he was in the fifth grade. It was a very exciting game, and Eddie scored the winning goal!

Now, Eddie plays basketball on the ninth-grade basketball team. Next year, he will try out for the tenth-grade soccer team as well. Then, he will be playing team sports practically all year round. When Eddie was five years old, his big sister took him to a college soccer game, and that's when he decided that he wanted to play on a sports team.

Today, his sister Jessica comes to his basketball games and claims that she inspired him to be the great athlete that he is. Eddie just laughs when she says that, but he does agree that she had a part in his love for athletics. Jessica frequently tells him that if he works hard, he can do anything. Eddie's most recent dream is to go to college on a basketball scholarship and study physics.

1. _____ Eddie plays on the ninth-grade basketball team.

2. _____ Eddie decided that he wanted to play on a sports team.

3. _____ Eddie's fifth-grade soccer team won the state championships.

4. _____ Eddie hopes to go to college and study physics.

5. _____ Eddie scored the winning goal for his fifth-grade soccer team.

6. _____ Eddie will try out for the tenth-grade soccer team.

Paragraph Maze

Friday Fun

Directions: Find your way through the maze by making a paragraph. Some words in the paragraph are written right to left and bottom to top, so read carefully!

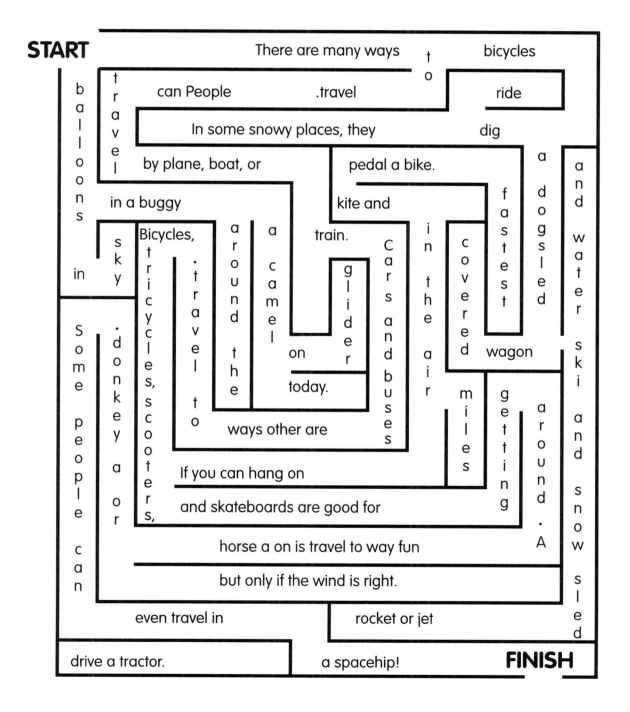

START

There are many ways to bicycles

t
r
a
v
e
l
  can People   .travel   ride

In some snowy places, they   dig

by plane, boat, or   pedal a bike.

in a buggy   kite and

b
a
l
l
o
o
n
s

in

Bicycles,   a camel   train.

Some people can

Cars and buses

covered miles   fastest   a dogsled

and water ski and snow sled

wagon

getting around. A

If you can hang on

and skateboards are good for

horse a on is travel to way fun

but only if the wind is right.

even travel in   rocket or jet

drive a tractor.   a spacehip!   FINISH

House Numbers

Directions: Read each clue to fill in the chart below. If the answer to the clue is "yes," make an **O** in the box. If the answer is "no," make an **X** in the box. Then, answer the statements below the chart.

Clues

- ✿ Marie's house number has only odd numbers in it.
- ✿ Jay's house number has more even numbers than odd numbers.
- ✿ Sean's house number is evenly divisible by 3.
- ✿ Larissa's house number is evenly divisible by 10.

	61	276	810	954	977
Jay					
Tina					
Larissa					
Sean					
Marie					

1. Jay's house number is _____.

2. Tina's house number is _____.

3. Larissa's house number is _____.

4. Sean's house number is _____.

5. Marie's house number is _____.

Reading Graphs

Math

Directions: Answer the questions about the graphs.

Types of Books Checked Out

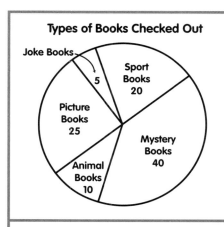

Joke Books
5
Sport Books 20
Picture Books 25
Mystery Books 40
Animal Books 10

1. How many books were checked out in all?

_____

2. Which type of book was checked out more than picture books?

_____

3. How many more students checked out mystery books than animal books?

_____

4. What is the least popular book?

_____

Which type of book is checked out the most?

_____

5. How many chocolate ice-cream cones were sold?

_____

6. Which flavor of ice-cream cone sold the most?

_____

7. How many more strawberry cones were sold than vanilla cones?

_____

8. How many ice-cream cones were sold in all?

_____

Ice-Cream Cones Sold on Sunday

Chocolate

Vanilla

Strawberry

Sherbet

🍦 = 10 cones

Story Detective

Directions: The following story gives you many clues about what Daryl and his family are planning to do. Read the story carefully, and then answer the questions below.

> Daryl couldn't believe the day was finally here! His mother woke him up early and rushed him to breakfast. "Make sure you wash your own bowl and put it back, Daryl," his mother said, "I don't want dirty dishes left behind." Daryl reached into a box filled with newspaper-wrapped dishes and pulled out a bowl for his breakfast.
>
> As Daryl finished washing his dish, his best friend, Larry, came to the back door. "Hey, Daryl! I thought I'd better bring this sweatshirt over to you," he explained. "You left it at my house a while back. It might be some time before I see you again."
>
> "Thanks," Daryl replied with a smile. "I wondered what happened to that."
>
> "Yeah, and you're probably going to really need it now," Larry stated. "No more beach clothes for you!"
>
> "Yeah," said Daryl, "but I'm ready for a change."

1. What can you infer from this story? What are Daryl and his family getting ready to do? (Be as specific as you can.)

   _____

   _____

   _____

2. What clues helped you to make this inference? List at least three specific clues from the story.

   _____

   _____

   _____

Money Math

Directions: Solve each problem.

1. $4.20 + $3.99	2. $28.99 + $41.35	3. $10.50 − $ 5.42

4. $58.14
− $26.25

5. $39.73
+ $17.41

6. $4.87 + $1.87	7. $10.23 + $ 7.64	8. $6.20 − $1.11

9. $8.23
− $2.50

10. Mrs. Mayberry bought pencils for $3.18, and Mrs. Penn bought notebooks for $8.76. How much money did they spend in all?

_____

What Is a Subject?

A **sentence** is a group of words that tell about something. A sentence tells about a person, place, thing, or idea. A **subject** of a sentence is who or what the sentence is about. See the example below.

The boy ran.

Who is this sentence about? This sentence is about the boy. The subject of this sentence is *the boy*.

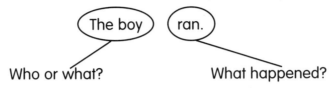

Directions: Read the following sentences, and see if you can find the subject of each sentence. Who or what is the sentence about? Circle the subject in each sentence.

1. The school was given the top rating.

2. The dog is attending obedience school.

3. The sun set on the horizon.

4. Fourth graders love to read.

5. Spring is coming.

Directions: Look at the subjects below. Write sentences using each of these subjects. Remember, the sentences must be about these subjects.

6. Lisa

_____

7. zoo

_____

8. peanuts

_____

9. bicycle

_____

10. airplane

_____

More Operations

Directions: Read each problem. Then, circle or write your answers on the lines. Show your work.

1. Into how many groups of 5 can the stars shown here be divided?

   a. 2 with 5 left over

   b. 3 with 3 left over

   c. 4 with 2 left over

   d. 5 with 3 left over

2. Kane bought 3 boxes of candy. There were 12 candy bars in each box. Four of the twelve candy bars had peanuts, and the rest had caramel. Each box cost $4.90. How many candy bars did Kane buy?

   _____

3. Lois charges $25 for each yard she mows. Over the summer, she mowed 63 yards. How much money did Lois earn?

   _____

4. Justin bought 8 cases of soda for his sister's party. There were 24 cans in each case. How many cans of soda did Justin buy altogether?

   _____

Mozart

Directions: Read the story, and then circle the correct answers below.

Mozart is one of the world's most famous composers. Mozart's music is so famous that it is used all over the world. How did Mozart come to write such beautiful music? Mozart was born in Austria. He was the son of a well-known composer and teacher. Mozart received lessons from his father and was playing before royalty and other important people by the age of six. By the time he was ten years old, Mozart had traveled and played music all over Europe.

It didn't take long for Mozart to begin writing music of his own. He wrote many musical works. Many people knew he was talented, but Mozart was not paid for writing music. He received money only when he would play. He was forced to give piano lessons to earn enough money to live.

It wasn't until 1780 when Mozart was finally paid to write music. He was given the job to write an opera. He produced his most famous work in the next three years. When Mozart died in 1791, he left a legacy of beautiful music that would impress crowds all over the world.

1. What is the author's purpose for writing this passage about Mozart?

    a. to share the facts about Mozart and his family

    b. to share the inspiring story of Mozart

    c. to point out that Mozart was not paid enough

    d. to list all works written by Mozart

2. Which sentence from the passage shows how the author feels about Mozart?

    a. He produced his most famous work in the next three years.

    b. How did Mozart come to write such beautiful music?

    c. He received money only when he would play.

    d. By the time he was ten years old, Mozart had traveled and played music all over Europe.

3. Which of the following statements did not happen?

    a. Mozart learned to play beautiful music at a very young age.

    b. Mozart was naturally talented and skilled.

    c. Mozart was paid to play for the president of the United States.

    d. Mozart left a legacy of music that is still played today.

Probability

Directions: Read each problem. Then, circle or write your answers on the cards.

1. Jake has a deck of cards with letters printed on them. He has 2 cards with an "A," 2 cards with a "B," 2 cards with a "C," and 3 cards with a "D." If he shuffles the cards and turns them over one at a time, what will the last card be?

D B D C A D B C

2. Linda has 5 ink pens in her purse. Two are black, 1 is green, and 2 are red. Which of the following combinations is NOT possible if Linda chooses 3 ink pens from her purse?

    a. 2 red and 1 green

    b. 1 green and 2 blue

    c. 2 black and 1 green

    d. 2 red and 1 black

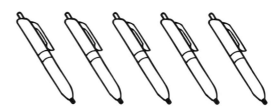

3. The table shows how many picture cards Jimmy has. Based on the table, what card will Jimmy turn over next?

Cat	2
Dog	3
Rabbit	2
Butterfly	2

a. butterfly   b. dog   c. cat   d. rabbit

What Is a Predicate?

Just as all sentences have a subject, they also have a predicate. A **predicate** tells important things about the subject. The predicate tells what the subject does, has, or is. In the sentence below, the word *ran* is the predicate. It explains what *the boy*, the subject, is doing.

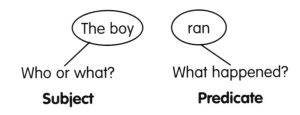

Who or what?   What happened?

Subject   **Predicate**

Directions: Draw a circle around the subject in each sentence below. Once you have located the subject in each of the sentences, underline the predicate. The first one has been done for you.

1. (The dog) jumped into the lake.

2. Everyone was laughing.

3. Erika has a cold.

4. The cat jumped off the log.

5. They ate the birthday cake.

6. She can do a backward flip.

7. Summer is the time for fishing.

Directions: Write sentences using the following predicates.

8. jumped into the water   _____

9. claps at the end   _____

10. eats hot dogs   _____

11. races the boys   _____

12. is happy   _____

13. sits on the bench   _____

14. always eats ketchup   _____

Tricky Shapes

Directions: Look at the figure below. How many triangles are there? _____
Hint: Don't forget to look for the upside-down triangles or the ones you can make by combining triangles.

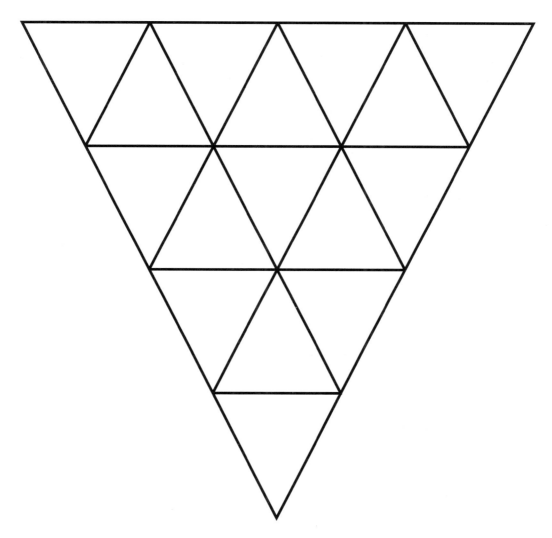

How many quadrilaterals are in the figure below? _____

Boggle the Mind

Directions: Look at the letters in the grids below. How many words can you think of using the given letters? Follow the rules below to find the answers. Two examples of words are given for the first grid.

Rules

✿ You must use the central letter of the grid as the beginning letter of each word.

✿ No letter can be used more than the number of times it is given.

✿ Letters do not need to be connected.

✿ No proper nouns or slang words allowed.

1.

L	O	D
B	**F**	N
I	L	D

_____ **Words** _____

fib

fill

2.

M	T	A
I	**L**	N
D	E	F

_____ **Words** _____

3.

L	A	B
I	**C**	R
L	S	T

_____ **Words** _____

Divide and Conquer

Directions: Do these problems. Use the multiplication chart on page 104 if you are unsure of your facts. The first two have been done for you.

1.
$$
\begin{array}{r}
122\ R5 \\
6\overline{)737} \\
-6 \\
\hline
13 \\
-12 \\
\hline
17 \\
-12 \\
\hline
5
\end{array}
$$

2.
$$
\begin{array}{r}
175\ R2 \\
3\overline{)527} \\
-3 \\
\hline
22 \\
-21 \\
\hline
17 \\
-15 \\
\hline
2
\end{array}
$$

3. $4\overline{)293}$

4. $4\overline{)531}$

5. $5\overline{)617}$

6. $2\overline{)193}$

7. $6\overline{)437}$

8. $8\overline{)239}$

9. $4\overline{)857}$

10. $6\overline{)273}$

11. $3\overline{)313}$

12. $7\overline{)629}$

Connecting Thoughts

> **Segues** (pronounced "seg-ways") and **transitions** are used to connect thoughts and ideas. The chart below contains a list of common segues and transitions.

Directions: Read the following sentences, and notice the segues and transitions used. Notice how they enhance the sentences. Note the comma use as well in some of the sentences.

- ☼ **Consequently,** the director decided to "cut" the scene.

- ☼ **Obviously,** the students had practiced their instruments quite a bit.

- ☼ **As a result** of reading the first book, I knew what to expect.

above	consequently	meanwhile
according to	even though	moreover
additionally	for instance	nevertheless
after	furthermore	next
along with	however	obviously
also	in addition to	of course
although	in conclusion	similarly
another	in fact	since
as a result	in summary	therefore
because	last	to emphasize
besides	lastly	while
clearly	likewise	yet

Now, write your own sentences using at least one segue or transition from above in each sentence.

1. _____

2. _____

3. _____

4. _____

5. _____

6. _____

Patterns

Directions: Read each problem. Then, circle or write your answers on the lines.

1. What should you do to find the next number in the pattern?

    a. add 9 to 158

    b. add 10 to 158

    c. subtract 10 from 158

    d. subtract 10 from 188

    188, 178, 168, 158, _____

2. Solve the problems below.

    $(10 \times 15) \div 5 =$ _____ $(6 \times 6) \div 2 =$ _____ $(7 \times 6) \div 2 =$ _____

    $(8 \div 4) \times 3 =$ _____ $(12 \div 4) \times 2 =$ _____ $(10 \div 2) \times 3 =$ _____

    $3 \times (15 \div 3) =$ _____ $3 \times (4 \div 4) =$ _____ $9 \times (15 \div 3) =$ _____

3. Dahlia folded her green, yellow, orange, and white T-shirts and placed them in her drawer.
    The green was on top of the white T-shirt. The orange was on top of all the other T-shirts. The
    yellow shirt was on top of the green shirt but under the orange shirt. List the order Dahlia
    placed her T-shirts in her drawer.

Top

Bottom

Letter from Belize

Directions: Carefully read the letter below, and then answer the following questions in complete sentences.

August 26, 2009

Dear Friend,

I regret to inform you that this will be the last letter that I will be able to write to you about Belize. There is still so much more left to tell you! I guess you will just have to do some research on your own to answer some of your remaining questions.

I decided that I must tell you something about some of the schools in Belize. The school that our friends' children attend is a private school. They have classes there from Infant 1 through Standard 4. This would be similar to U.S. schools that have kindergarten through fifth grade classes. The students and teachers wear uniforms at the school, but this is true of all of the schools in Belize. Some schools have as long as one and a half hours for lunch breaks, and many of the students go home to eat lunch. At recess, many of the girls play jacks, and they are very good at it!

Belize has a lot of great sites and new things to experience, and it will be sad to leave when our trip is over. Of course, what I will miss the most is my new friends and my old friends in Belize. Fortunately, though, we can keep in contact through letters and e-mail. I also predict that since I love Belize and my friends so much, I will be back to visit again many times in my life.

So long,

Julia

---

1. What is one prediction you can make about what you think Julia would write next if she were to write another letter? What makes you think that?

   _____

   _____

   _____

2. Why is it important for readers to make predictions while they read?

   _____

   _____

Averages

Week 4: Wednesday

Directions: Calculate the average for each of the problems. The first one has been started for you.

1. Shawna had 3 math grades: 80, 90, and 100. What was her average math grade?

$$\frac{80 + 90 + 100}{3} =$$

Her average math grade was _____.

2. James had 3 science grades: 60, 70, and 80. What was his average science grade?

His average science grade was _____.

3. Susan had 4 social studies grades: 93, 86, 70, and 71. What was her average social studies grade?

Her average social studies grade was _____.

4. The weights of 5 puppies were 12 pounds, 39 pounds, 15 pounds, 24 pounds, and 30 pounds. What was their average weight?

Their average weight was _____ pounds.

5. The weights of 5 rocks were 12 pounds, 48 pounds, 18 pounds, 32 pounds, and 35 pounds. What was the average weight?

The average weight was _____ pounds.

6. In the zoo, the weights of 6 bears were 57 pounds, 130 pounds, 99 pounds, 97 pounds, 88 pounds, and 63 pounds. What was their average weight?

Their average weight was _____ pounds.

Questions

Directions: Write a question for each of the following answers. The first one has been done for you.

1. **Question:** _What natural occurrence happens when the ground shakes?_

   Answer: an earthquake

2. **Question:** _____

   Answer: the giraffe and the zebra

3. **Question:** _____

   Answer: $1,349.90

4. **Question:** _____

   Answer: London, England

5. **Question:** _____

   Answer: apricots, apples, and apes

6. **Question:** _____

   Answer: a marathon

7. **Question:** _____

   Answer: *Mona Lisa*

8. **Question:** _____

   Answer: *The Nutcracker*

9. **Question:** _____

   Answer: *Romeo and Juliet*

10. **Question:** _____

    Answer: a turtle

11. **Question:** _____

    Answer: every fourth Wednesday

Rounding and More

Directions: For problems 1–4, round to the nearest 10. For problems 5–8, round to the nearest 100. For problems 9–10, solve the problems.

1. 42 _____	2. 78 _____	3. 56 _____

4. 186 _____	5. 5,329 _____

6. 864 _____	7. 729 _____	8. 671 _____

9. Daniel saw 16 trees, 12 bushes, 23 flowers, and 2 lizards on his walk in the woods. How many items did Daniel see?

_____

10. Greta is 6 years younger than her brother. Her brother is 13. How old is Greta?

_____

Given a Chance

Directions: Find the meaning of each underlined word in the nonfiction story below. Using the definitions box, put the letter of the answer on the blank line.

> a. to give pay in exchange for work   d. voted in, chosen
>
> b. a member of a group or squad   e. something that stops or restricts
>
> c. needed

1. ____

2. ____

3. ____

4. ____

5. ____

Marion Motley just wanted a chance to do what he did best: play football. Marion Motley was an African American, and for a long time, no professional football teams wanted to ¹employ African Americans. Finally, at the age of 26, Motley was given a chance to try out for one team, the Cleveland Browns. The year was 1946—one year before Jackie Robinson broke the color ²barrier in baseball. Motley made the team, and he went on to be one of the greatest players in football history. He was a big, fast, tough runner who led the league in rushing in 1948 and 1950. He was also a great blocker who risked getting hurt in order to protect his team's quarterback. This was one of the reasons why Motley was known as a great ³teammate; he would do whatever was ⁴necessary to help his team win. And the Browns won a lot! From 1946–1950, the Browns won five straight championships. In 1968, Motley became the second African American to be ⁵elected to the Pro Football Hall of Fame.

Directions: Decide if the following pairs are synonyms (same meaning) or antonyms (opposite meaning). Write **S** (for *synonym*) or **A** (for *antonym*) in each blank.

6. employ   hire   _____

7. barrier   opening   _____

8. teammate   enemy   _____

9. necessary   required   _____

10. elected   refused   _____

Calots and Wiggles

Directions: Complete the page after evaluating the examples below.

1. These figures are *calots*.

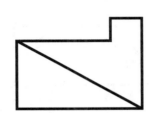

2. None of these are *calots*.

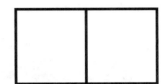

3. What makes something a *calot*? According to your definition, draw three other figures that are *calots*.

4. These figures are *wiggles*.

5. None of these are *wiggles*.

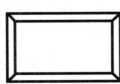 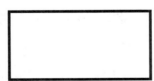 

6. What makes something a *wiggle*? According to your definition, draw three other figures that are *wiggles*.

Different Sports

Directions: Do you participate on a sports team? The six children in this chart each compete in a different sport. From the clues below, determine the sport that each child plays. Mark the correct boxes with a **Y** for *yes* and the incorrect boxes with an **N** for *no*.

	Soccer	Basketball	Volleyball	Baseball	Swimming	Track
Anne						
Elise						
Ethan						
Katie						
Kevin						
Logan						

Clues

☼ Ethan needs water to compete.

☼ Anne's sport requires knee pads.

☼ Elise dribbles a ball with her hands.

☼ Katie's sport begins and ends with the same letters as Elise's sport.

☼ Logan is a goalie.

☼ Kevin runs in circles.

Terms and More

Directions: For problems 1–8, circle the correct term for the underlined part of each number sentence. Then, solve problems 9 and 10.

---

1. <u>81</u> divided by 9 = 9

   a. minuend
   b. addend
   c. multiplier
   d. dividend

2. 6 x <u>6</u> = 36

   a. subtrahend
   b. addend
   c. multiplier
   d. dividend

3. <u>33</u> – 11 = 22

   a. minuend
   b. addend
   c. multiplier
   d. dividend

---

4. <u>10 + 10</u> = 20

   a. subtrahends
   b. addends
   c. multipliers
   d. divisors

5. 3 x 5 = <u>15</u>

   a. product
   b. sum
   c. difference
   d. quotient

---

6. 10 – 8 = <u>2</u>

   a. product
   b. sum
   c. difference
   d. quotient

7. 23 + 23 = <u>46</u>

   a. product
   b. sum
   c. difference
   d. quotient

8. 20 ÷ 5 = <u>4</u>

   a. product
   b. sum
   c. difference
   d. quotient

---

9. It takes 24 inches of string to wrap a package. How much string will be needed to wrap 25 packages?

   _____

10. Cleveland has a population of 104,238; Columbus has a population of 679,234; and Dayton has a population of 414,757. What is the total population of all three cities?

    _____

Lena

Directions: Read the story and then record facts from it that give you clues as to what Lena's job is. Finally, make an inference about what Lena's job is.

> When Lena entered her office, she put down her briefcase and anxiously listened to her voicemail messages. She jotted down the phone numbers of the three people who had called, grabbed her notebook and pen, and dialed the first number on her list. "Wow! Really? They found it in the backyard? Now, that's news!" she said. Lena asked the caller a series of questions and feverishly took notes as the person answered the questions. After making all of her calls, Lena began typing the information she had gained. "This'll be great for the front page!" she exclaimed.

Clues *(facts from the story)*

_____

_____

_____

_____

_____

Inference *(conclusion about what Lena's job is)*

_____

_____

_____

_____

_____

Add Signs and Solve

Directions: Place the ÷ sign and the = sign in the squares so that each number sentence is correct.

1. 48 ☐ 6 ☐ 8

2. 100 ☐ 10 ☐ 10

3. 18 ☐ 2 ☐ 9

4. 55 ☐ 5 ☐ 11

5. 63 ☐ 9 ☐ 7

6. 14 ☐ 7 ☐ 2

7. 25 ☐ 5 ☐ 5

8. 56 ☐ 7 ☐ 8

9. 36 ☐ 12 ☐ 3

Directions: Place the division sign, the equal sign, and the answer in the correct order.

10. 42 ☐ 6 ☐ _____

11. 9 ☐ 3 ☐ _____

12. 21 ☐ 7 ☐ _____

13. 36 ☐ 6 ☐ _____

14. 10 ☐ 2 ☐ _____

15. 28 ☐ 4 ☐ _____

16. 45 ☐ 5 ☐ _____

17. 6 ☐ 6 ☐ _____

18. 32 ☐ 8 ☐ _____

Directions: Solve and watch out for any remainders.

19. $28 \div 6 =$ _____ R _____

20. $8 \div 6 =$ _____ R _____

21. $28 \div 9 =$ _____ R _____

22. $17 \div 8 =$ _____ R _____

23. $14 \div 3 =$ _____ R _____

24. $15 \div 7 =$ _____ R _____

25. $21 \div 10 =$ _____ R _____

26. $16 \div 9 =$ _____ R _____

27. $23 \div 5 =$ _____ R _____

28. $26 \div 3 =$ _____ R _____

29. $28 \div 10 =$ _____ R _____

30. $29 \div 4 =$ _____ R _____

All About Capitals

Directions: The following sentences need capitalization. Underline each letter that should be changed to a capital three times, and write the capital letter above the underlined letter.

Example: i went to new york on saturday.

1. when i went to the store, i saw my teacher, mrs. roe.

2. my family will go to disneyland in july.

3. i am reading <u>old yeller</u> this week.

4. my sister sarah says her favorite subject is spanish.

5. on wednesday, we will celebrate groundhog day.

6. my brother said that mom was a cheerleader at eastside high school.

7. in august, we're going to visit aunt mary in san francisco, california.

8. benji had a birthday, so she sang "happy birthday to you."

9. my friend rosa speaks spanish, and i speak english.

10. my neighbor julia is going to paris, france, next june.

Differences

Math

Directions: Find the differences between the times. Estimate first, and then find the actual answer.

	Starting Time	Finishing Time	Estimate	Actual Answer
1.	9:30 a.m.	11:15 a.m.		
2.	10:09 a.m.	11:11 a.m.		
3.	7:45 a.m.	8:50 a.m.		
4.	10:00 a.m.	12:51 p.m.		
5.	3:35 p.m.	6:42 p.m.		
6.	8:25 p.m.	11:05 p.m.		
7.	1:07 a.m.	4:45 a.m.		
8.	2:35 a.m.	6:55 a.m.		

Directions: Estimate how long it takes to do the following things. Compare your answers with someone in your house.

9. brush your teeth _____

10. eat lunch _____

11. travel to school _____

12. get dressed _____

13. tie your shoelaces _____

14. complete your homework _____

15. pack your lunch _____

16. sharpen your pencil _____

The Crash

Directions: Read the story carefully. Follow the directions for each question, and then answer the questions in complete sentences.

> It was a bright and sunny day when Jessica got into the car. She rolled down the window and turned up the radio. Jessica could not believe that her father was finally letting her drive his car. Jessica had gotten her driver's license a month ago, but her dad was very protective of his car and refused to let her drive it anywhere. Today, however, her father was in an especially happy mood and agreed that she could use his car for the afternoon. Now, Jessica was happily headed to her best friend Jacquie's house.
>
> As Jessica pulled out of the driveway, her favorite song came on, so she turned up the volume of the radio. Just as she pulled onto the road, a dog ran out in the middle of the street. Jessica swerved to miss the dog and ended up running into the neighbors' trash cans. "Oh, no!" Jessica thought. "Now Dad will never let me drive his car again!"

1. Underline the sentence in the story that says Jessica's father agreed to let her use his car for the afternoon.

   What caused Jessica's father to let her drive his car for the afternoon? _____

   _____

   _____

   _____

2. Underline the sentence in the story that says Jessica turned up the volume of the radio.

   What caused Jessica to turn up the volume of the radio? _____

   _____

   _____

3. Underline the sentence in the story that says Jessica swerved the car.

   What caused Jessica to swerve? _____

   _____

   _____

Decimals and Fractions

Directions: For problems 1–6, write each fraction as a decimal. For problems 7–8, write each decimal as a fraction. Then, solve problems 9–10.

1.

$$\frac{6}{10} = \underline{\hspace{2cm}}$$

2.

$$\frac{4}{10} = \underline{\hspace{2cm}}$$

3.

$$\frac{9}{100} = \underline{\hspace{2cm}}$$

4. forty-eight and seven hundredths

_____

5.

$$2\frac{7}{10} = \underline{\hspace{3cm}}$$

6. nine and three tenths

_____

7.

$$0.7 = \underline{\hspace{2cm}}$$

8.

$$0.2 = \underline{\hspace{2cm}}$$

9. The Watsons had a pizza for supper. It was divided into 8 slices. Joey, his mom, and his dad each had $\frac{1}{4}$ of the pizza. How many slices did each person eat?

_____

10. If you could only buy one shirt, and the price was two for $12.50, how much would one shirt cost?

_____

More Cause and Effect

> **Cause** and **effect** explains why an event occurred by telling the results of an action.

Directions: List four possible causes for each of the following effects.

A teenager is grounded for a whole week.

1. _____

2. _____

3. _____

4. _____

Several farm animals have wandered away from the farm.

1. _____

2. _____

3. _____

4. _____

Local police officers have closed a bridge.

1. _____

2. _____

3. _____

4. _____

A short boy is made captain of the basketball team.

1. _____

2. _____

3. _____

4. _____

Gymnastic Rebus

Directions: Decode the picture and letter clues to reveal gymnastics terms.

1. _____ _____

2. _____ _____   F +

3. _____   P +   – B

4. _____   T +   – D

5. _____ _____   ST +   – H   + S

6. _____ _____   Pom +   – CA

7. _____ _____   B +   – ST

8. _____ _____ _____   – S

Idiom Crossword

Directions: To complete the idiom, fill in the blanks with the words in the Word Bank. Then, use the missing words to complete the crossword puzzle. "3 Down" has been done for you.

Word Bank

bed	roof
bone	shoulder
ceiling	stack
crazy	throat
goat	~~warpath~~
handle	

Across

2. Have a _____ to pick with you—to have an argument or try to settle a disagreement with someone
4. Jump down your _____—to talk or scream at someone in an angry way
6. Drive you _____—to annoy or irritate someone
7. Get up on the wrong side of the _____—to get up in the morning in a bad mood
8. Chip on your _____—not able to forgive

Down

1. Get your _____—to annoy or irritate
3. On the ___warpath___—angry and upset
5. Get a _____ on something—to have control of something
6. Hit the _____—to become very angry
8. Blow your _____—to become very angry
9. Go through the _____—to go very high or reach a high degree (e.g., temperature)

60

Measure Up

Directions: Determine the measurement for each item. Multiply the number of meters by 39 (inches), and then divide that number by 12 to get the answer. Round each answer to the nearest foot.

1. The first sprint in the 776 B.C. Olympics was 192 meters long.

   192 meters = _____ feet

2. "World's Fastest Human" is the title given the winner of the 100-meter sprint.

   100 meters = _____ feet

3. Male athletes run 110-meter hurdles.

   110 meters = _____ feet

4. A popular indoor race is 60 meters long.

   60 meters = _____ feet

5. The 1500-meter race is known as the metric mile. However, the measurement is not exactly a mile. Find the difference between a standard mile (5,280 feet) and a metric mile.

   1500 meters = _____ feet

   The difference between a metric mile and a standard mile is _____ feet.

Directions: Read the information about these track and field recordholders. Convert the measurements from feet to meters to the nearest hundredth. Multiply the number of feet by 12, and then divide by 39 to get the answer.

6. Al Oerter, from the United States, was the first man to throw the discus more than 200 feet.

   200 feet = _____ meters

7. Sergei Bubka, from the Ukraine, was the first pole vaulter to clear 20 feet.

   20 feet = _____ meters

8. Randy Barnes, from the United States, holds the standing outdoor shot put record with a throw of 75 feet.

   75 feet = _____ meters

Terrific Titles

> ## Punctuation Rules
> When punctuating titles, italicize or underline the titles of books, professional journals, plays, TV shows, movies, and magazines. For shorter works, such as articles, short stories, and poems, punctuate the titles with quotation marks.

Directions: Punctuate the titles correctly within the sentences.

1. I really enjoyed reading the book Chato and the Party Animals by Gary Soto.

2. One of the best poems I have ever read is Years Later by Lawrence Raab.

3. The TV show Glee has very likeable characters.

4. I read an article entitled Dogs Are Man's Best Friend in a magazine recently.

5. We went to see the Broadway musical Wicked.

6. The book 20,000 Leagues Under the Sea by Jules Verne is packed with adventure.

7. In the movie Up, the main character ties balloons to his house and flies away.

8. This weekend, we went to see the play The Wizard of Oz.

9. Robert Frost wrote the poem The Road Not Taken.

10. In The Indian in the Cupboard series, Lynn Reid Banks stimulates the readers' imaginations.

Match and Expand

Directions: Expand these numbers. An example has been done for you.

Example: 2,641 = 2,000 + 600 + 40 + 1

1. 561 = _____

2. 9,011 = _____

3. 3,587 = _____

4. 4,404 = _____

5. 826 = _____

6. 8,990 = _____

Directions: Match the following numbers. The first one has been done for you.

7. 3,659 $(1 \times 1,000) + (2 \times 10) + (8 \times 1)$

8. 590   six one-hundreds

9. 1,028   800 + 70 + 5

10. 84   3 thousands + 5 hundreds + 15 tens + 9 ones

11. 600   no ones, no tens, three hundreds, two thousands

12. 2,300   seven ones, three tens, four hundreds, nine thousands

13. 875   nineteen hundreds, two ones

14. 9,437   five hundreds, eight tens, ten ones

15. 1,902   seven tens, fourteen ones

Directions: Write these numbers in standard form. Be careful of the place values!

16. 10 + 1,000 + 300 + 6 = _____

17. 9 + 600 + 40 = _____

18. 400 + 4,000 + 6 = _____

19. 2,000 + 3 = _____

20. 6 + 800 + 40 = _____

21. 40 + 9,000 + 1 = _____

22. 90 + 7,000 + 5 = _____

23. 3 + 700 + 20 + 1,000 = _____

24. 1,000 + 4 + 60 + 100 = _____

25. 5,000 + 0 = _____

It's Alive!

> **Personification** is a figure of speech that portrays an animal, object, or idea as if it had human qualities.

Directions: Read each sentence. Underline the personification, and then circle the sentence that best gives the real meaning of this figure of speech. The first one has been done for you.

1. An old jalopy <u>gagged and wheezed</u> as it tried to climb the steep hill.
   a. The car's driver was choking.
   b. The car has run over something in the road.
   ⓒ The car's motor is making a lot of noise.

2. Curiosity ate away at Denise until she finally asked if the winning ticket was hers.
   a. Denise has a terrible skin disease.
   b. Denise could not stop thinking about her ticket.
   c. Denise was being chewed upon by an animal.

3. Fog huddled all along the docks of the bay.
   a. You could not see the water because of the fog.
   b. You are at a football game near a lake.
   c. You are out in the rain without an umbrella.

4. Gusty winds made a leaf pile hop, skip, and jump.
   a. The leaves were blowing around.
   b. The leaves were dancing in the street.
   c. The leaves were being raked.

5. The cave seemed to yawn as explorers went inside.
   a. The explorers were very tired.
   b. The explorers were searching for a place to camp.
   c. The explorers were going through a large opening.

6. Prickly bushes grabbed at me as I walked through the thick weeds.
   a. There were prickly bushes that had claws.
   b. There were thorns on the bushes that scratched me.
   c. There were evil people hiding in the weeds.

7. There is not much traffic in that sleepy, little town.
   a. The town is quiet.
   b. The townspeople are good sleepers.
   c. The town has no roads.

Just Round It

Directions: Round the following numbers to the nearest 10.

1. 15 = _____

2. 42 = _____

3. 82 = _____

4. 22 = _____

5. 55 = _____

6. 19 = _____

7. 39 = _____

8. 63 = _____

9. 35 = _____

10. 11 = _____

11. 78 = _____

12. 41 = _____

Directions: Round the following numbers to the nearest 100.

13. 152 = _____

14. 310 = _____

15. 425 = _____

16. 130 = _____

17. 450 = _____

18. 721 = _____

19. 267 = _____

20. 683 = _____

21. 888 = _____

22. 280 = _____

23. 790 = _____

24. 901 = _____

Directions: Round the following numbers to the nearest 1,000.

25. 3,267 = _____

26. 5,555 = _____

27. 7,136 = _____

28. 4,500 = _____

29. 2,230 = _____

30. 8,917 = _____

31. 1,644 = _____

32. 7,896 = _____

33. 6,499 = _____

34. 7,320 = _____

35. 6,200 = _____

36. 7,501 = _____

Make It Interesting

A **topic sentence** states the main idea and must capture a reader's interest.

Directions: Read the following list of writing ideas. Create a topic sentence for each.

1. the best place to go swimming _____

   _____

2. my favorite amusement park ride _____

   _____

3. enjoyable board games to play _____

   _____

4. our family's most valuable possession _____

   _____

5. staying overnight at grandmother's house _____

   _____

6. the surprise party _____

   _____

Directions: Read the following topic sentences. Rewrite each in the form of a question, command, or exclamation.

7. Our vacation on a tropical island was very exciting. _____

   _____

8. I made too many mistakes on the first day of school. _____

   _____

9. A police car pulled into our driveway. _____

   _____

10. My parents brought home twins from the hospital. _____

    _____

Mixed Patterns

Math

Directions: Complete these number patterns.

1. 3, 19, 16, 3, 19, 16, _____ , 19, _____ , 3, _____ , _____ , 3, _____ , 16, _____ , _____ , _____

2. 35, 40, 16, 35, _____ , 16, _____ , _____ , _____ 35, _____ , _____ , _____ , _____ , _____

3. 1, 2, 2, 1, 2, _____ , _____ , 2, _____ , 1, _____ , _____ , 1, 2, _____ , _____ , 2, _____

4. 6, 7, 8, 6, _____ , _____ , _____ , 7, _____ , 6, _____ , _____ , _____ , 7, _____ , _____

5. 9, 19, 29, 39, 9, _____ , _____ , 39, _____ , _____ , 29, _____ , 9, _____ , _____ , _____

Directions: Complete these picture patterns.

6. △ , ○ , □ , △ , ___ , ___ , ___ , ___ , □ , △ , ___ , ___ , ___ , ○ , ___ , △

7. → , ↑ , ← , → , ___ , ___ , ___ , ↑ , ___ , ___ , ___ , ← , ___ , ___ , ___ , ←

8. ♡ , ♡ , ○ , □ , ♡ , ___ , ○ , ___ , ♡ , ♡ , ___ , ___ , ___ , ○ , ___ , ♡

9. ○ , ○ , ○ , △ , ○ , ___ , ___ , △ , ___ , ___ , ___ , ○ , ___ , ___ , ___ , ○

10. □ , ▯ , □ , ▯ , ___ , ___ , ___ , ___ , ___ , ▯ , ___ , ___ , □ , ___ , ___

Directions: Look at each pattern and complete the tables.

11. △ , △▽ , △▽△

Number of triangles	1	2	3	6	8	11
Number of sides						

12. ⊙ , ⊙⊙ , ⊙⊙⊙

Number of circles	1	2	3	7	9	12
Number of dots						

Puppy Love

Directions: Read the story, and then circle the correct answers below.

It wasn't the prettiest dog around, but it was a puppy. No matter the breed, a puppy is always cute. Gretchen had wanted a dog for as long as she could remember, but her parents had always said no. This time was different. The puppy had been hanging around their house for two days. It whimpered and seemed hungry. On the second night, Gretchen fed it some of her hot dog. It hadn't left her side since.

The next morning, Gretchen's parents called the animal shelter and reported the missing puppy. They were told that if no one claimed the puppy in 72 hours, the puppy could be theirs. They didn't seem too worried. They knew the owner would show up.

Two days went by without a call. On the third day, it happened. Everyone froze. Gretchen's father answered the phone. Whew! It wasn't the shelter. Thirty minutes later, the phone rang again. Gretchen **gasped** for air. It was someone selling soaps. Late in the evening, the phone rang again. This time it was the shelter.

The owner showed up at Gretchen's house the next morning. Gretchen hadn't slept at all that night. She couldn't believe it was over. But the owner asked if the family would be interested in adopting the puppy. Gretchen couldn't believe her ears. This was the last pup in the litter. They had been trying to find an owner. The smiles on her parents' faces made Gretchen realize that she was the proud owner of little Miracle.

1. What is this passage mainly about?

    a. how a puppy can get lost

    b. the process an owner takes to find a lost animal

    c. the different types of dogs

    d. how Gretchen finally received a dog

2. In the third paragraph, what does the word *gasped* mean?

    a. quickly took in air

    b. documented

    c. measured

    d. opened

3. What improved Gretchen's chances of finally getting a dog?

    a. A puppy is hard to house train.

    b. An adorable puppy is hard to refuse.

    c. An adorable puppy is hard to sell.

    d. Her parents realized how much Gretchen wanted a dog.

4. Why did Gretchen name her puppy Miracle?

    a. It was a miracle the puppy had not died.

    b. Her parents believe in miracles.

    c. It was a miracle that Gretchen's parents let her keep the dog.

    d. She had always wanted to name a dog Miracle.

Mail Muddle-Up

Directions: Figure out who got what, from whom, and with what stamp.

Andre, Ben, Cindy, and Daphne's mail is in the mailbox. There is a package, a postcard, a bill, and a letter (not necessarily in order). They have been sent by a mom, a dad, a baker, and an aunt (also not necessarily in order). Three items have stamps, each with one of the following pictures: Mount Rushmore, a penguin, and the Capitol building. One item has no stamp. Use the clues below to discover who got what from which sender and with what stamp. Write your answers on the lines below.

Clues

- ☼ Andre's mail was not a postcard, didn't come from his mom, and had no stamp.

- ☼ Cindy passed on the package with the penguin stamp to the correct person.

- ☼ One person was jealous because she only got a postcard, while her sister got a package.

- ☼ The dad put the wrong child's name on the mail.

- ☼ One person's mail, sender, and stamp were alliterative with that person's name!

1. Andre's mail was a _____ from _____

   with (a) _____ stamp.

2. Ben's mail was a_____ from _____

   with (a) _____ stamp.

3. Cindy's mail was a _____ from _____

   with (a) _____ stamp.

4. Daphne's mail was a _____ from _____

   with (a) _____ stamp.

Bicycle Word Search

Week 6: Friday   **Friday Fun**

Directions: Lots of bits make up a bike—and they're hidden "wheely well." Find the following words in the word search below.

air	BMX	handlebar	mudguard	pump	sprocket	valve
bell	chain	light	oil	seat	tire	wheel
bicycle	gears	mirror	pedal	spoke	tube	

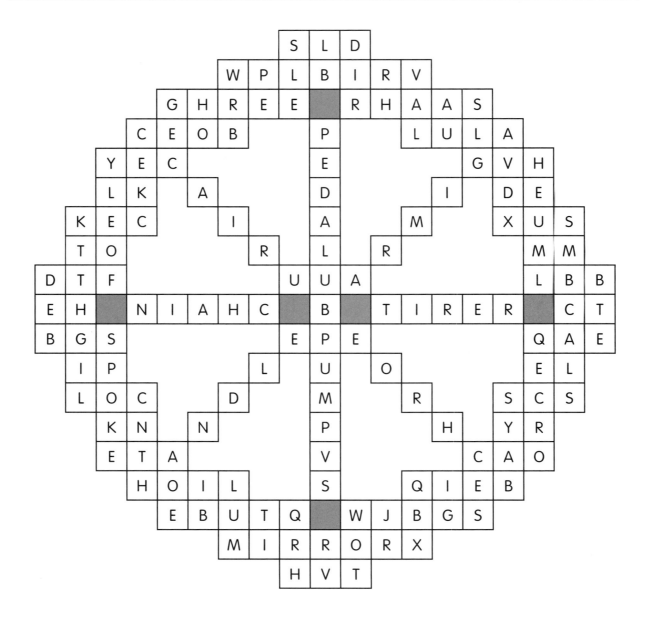

So Many Variables

Directions: Which equation could help you solve each problem? Write the letter of the correct equation in front of the problem, and then solve the equation on the line. Not all of the equations will be used.

> a. $21 \div 3 = x$
> b. $11 - 4 = p$
> c. $31 + 14 = b$
> d. $100 + v = 113$
> e. $12 - p = 4$
> f. $25 + s = 42$
> g. $21 \times 3 = c$
> h. $8 \times 7 = b$

_____ 1. Karl had 25 stamps in his collection. His uncle sent him some stamps. Karl now has 42 stamps. How many stamps did Karl's uncle send him? _____

_____ 2. Debbie packed 8 books in each box. She packed 7 boxes. How many books did she pack? _____

_____ 3. Mike's mom made 21 sandwiches for the picnic. She put 3 in each sack. How many sacks did she use? _____

_____ 4. April's dog had 12 puppies. April gave some away to her friends. Now, she has 4 puppies. How many puppies did she give away? _____

_____ 5. Elisa had 100 videos. Then, she bought some more. Now, she has 113 videos. How many videos did Elisa buy? _____

Directions: Find the value of each expression.

6. If r equals 4, what is the value of $r + 6$? _____

7. What is the value of $36 \div s$ if s equals 9? _____

8. What is the value of $t - 15$ if t equals 21? _____

9. If m equals 33, what is the value of $68 - m$? _____

10. What is the value of $b + 42$ if b equals 27? _____

Housework

Directions: Read the selection, and then answer the questions.

Once there was a mother mouse. She was very proud of her five mouse children. The mouse family lived in the house of a human family. The mouse family worked hard to keep the human home clean. After each meal, the mice would scurry out to pick up crumbs and other things that had dropped to the floor.

It was a busy and **hectic** life, but this was a hardworking mouse family. That is, except for one family member. Mina Mouse was content to spend her days lying around. She had no desire to work and managed to get out of most of the chores.

One day, Mother Mouse knew that things had to change! She sat Mina down and explained that she had to start carrying her own weight.

"But Mother," protested Mina.

"No, my child. You will one day see the wisdom in this," replied Mother Mouse.

And that day was soon to come. The next morning, Mother gave out assignments. The mice children hurried to get their jobs done so that they could play—that is, except for Mina. She spent her morning complaining.

Suddenly, there was a knock at the door. Mother answered the door and found her neighbor inviting the children to go with them to the circus. Mother allowed all her children to go as long as their chores were done. Everyone had their chores done . . . except for Mina. From that day forward, Mina always managed to get her jobs done first.

1. What did Mother Mouse mean when she talked to Mina about "carrying her own weight"?

   _____

   _____

2. What is the meaning of the word *hectic* as used in the story?

   a. chilly

   b. frantic

   c. disruptive

   d. calm

3. What is the moral of this story?

   a. A bird in the hand is worth two in the bush.

   b. A friend in need is a friend indeed.

   c. Work before play.

What's the Time?

Week 7: Tuesday

Math

Directions: Write the times from the list below on the digital clocks. Then, draw the hands showing the times on the analog clocks. The first one has been done for you.

1. twelve minutes past seven
2. six forty-four
3. ten twenty-five
4. six minutes before five
5. twenty-three minutes before three
6. eleven seventeen
7. two thirty-three
8. eighteen minutes after eight

Adjective Attention

An **adjective** describes a noun or pronoun. Adjectives usually answer the question *what kind* or *how many.*

Directions: Decide if the adjectives answer the question *what kind* or *how many.* Write your answer on the line.

1. all _____
2. best _____
3. few _____
4. new _____
5. warm _____
6. blue _____
7. fast _____

8. long _____
9. seven _____
10. white _____
11. a lot _____
12. eight _____
13. funny _____
14. million _____

Directions: Tell if the boldfaced adjectives answer the question *what kind* or *how many.*

15. There were **six** birds in our tree. _____

16. **Small** sparrows are good singers. _____

17. Blue jays eat **lots** of acorns and nuts. _____

18. An **old** crow sat on a dead branch._____

Directions: Circle all the adjectives that answer the question *what kind* or *how many.*

19. People, young and old, enjoy watching birds.

20. The only equipment you need is a pair of eyes.

21. Good ears and a guide book are helpful, too.

22. Experienced bird watchers use powerful binoculars.

Directions: Read each sentence. Underline adjectives that tell *what kind* once and adjectives that tell *how many* twice.

23. Find a quiet spot in a wooded area.

24. After several minutes, curious birds will visit you.

25. You should keep a record of the different birds in a small notebook.

Shapes and Angles

Words to Know

Polygon—a closed, two-dimensional figure with three or more straight lines

Quadrilateral—a polygon with four sides and four corners

Right angle—an angle that forms a square corner; a 90° angle

Directions: Color in all of the quadrilaterals.

  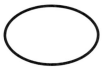 

 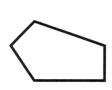

Directions: Draw squares on all of the right angles. The first one has been done for you.

 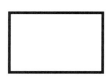  

Limericks

> **Limericks** are poems that are usually funny and have a regular rhythm (beat) and a regular pattern of rhyming words. Limericks are a popular kind of humorous verse.

Directions: Read the limericks, and then complete the activities.

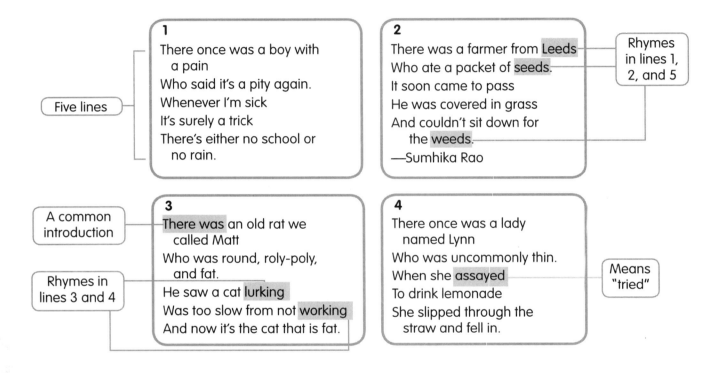

1. Circle the correct answer. The sick boy feels . . .

   a. cheated.   b. that life is unfair.   c. both a and b

2. Explain how you think the man from Leeds ended up unable to sit down because of "the weeds."

   _____

   _____

3. Write one sentence explaining what happened to Matt the rat.

   _____

4. Write one sentence explaining what happened to Lynn.

   _____

Read the Graphs

Directions: This line graph shows the cost of grapes. Use it to answer the questions.

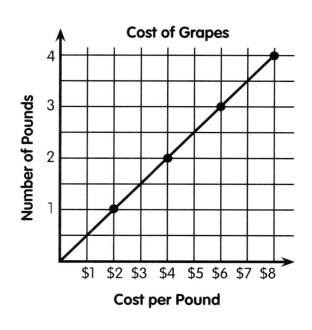

Cost of Grapes

Number of Pounds

$1 $2 $3 $4 $5 $6 $7 $8

Cost per Pound

1. How much will 1 pound of grapes cost?

   _____

2. How much will 3 pounds of grapes cost?

   _____

3. How many pounds of grapes could you buy for $7? _____

4. How many pounds of grapes could you buy for $1? _____

5. If you spent $5, what would your grapes weigh? _____

6. How much will it cost to buy 3½ pounds of grapes? _____

Directions: This line graph shows the number of DVDs borrowed over one week. Use it to answer the questions.

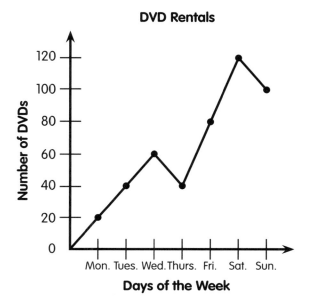

DVD Rentals

Number of DVDs

120
100
80
60
40
20
0

Mon. Tues. Wed. Thurs. Fri. Sat. Sun.

Days of the Week

7. What are the two busiest days at the DVD shop? _____

8. On which day was the least number of DVDs rented? _____

9. What day did the DVD shop rent out 100 DVDs? _____

10. How many DVDs did the shop rent out altogether? _____

What's the Order?

Directions: Put each group into its proper sequence.

	Morning Routine
eat	1.
wake	2.
dress	3.
wash	4.
brush teeth	5.

	How Jenny Got Stuck in a Tree
Jenny climbed higher.	6.
The cat climber higher.	7.
The cat raced up the tree.	8.
The dog chased Jenny's cat.	9.
The cat wouldn't come down.	10.
Jenny climbed the tree.	11.
Both were too frightened to climb down.	12.

Directions: Choose two of the following topics, and write a sequence of events for each.

> ☼ When I fell in the river   ☼ When the truck tipped over   ☼ When I spilled the milk

13. _____

_____

_____

_____

14. _____

_____

_____

_____

What Comes Next?

Week 7: Friday

Directions: Draw the next shape in each series.

1. ○ □ □ ○ □ □ ○ □	
2. ♡ △ △ ♡ △ △ ♡ △	
3. ○ ☆ ○ ☆ ○ ☆ ○ ☆	
4. □ □ □ D D D ♡ ♡	
5. ○ △ ○ ▽ ○ △ ○ ▽	
6. ≡ ☆ □ ≡ ☆ □ ≡ ☆	
7. □ △ △ ♡ ♡ ♡ D D D	
8. △ △ ○ ○ △ △ □ □ △	
9. ♡ ♡ ☆ ♡ ♡ □ ♡ ♡ ☆ ♡	
10. □ ▭ □ ▭ □ ▭ □ ▭ □	

Reverse Words

Directions: Reverse words are words that become different words when read backwards. Write the words and their reverses from the clues below.

Example: physician/fish = doc/cod

1. sticky substance/rodent _____

2. not cooked/battle _____

3. cooking container/the best _____

4. cat and dog/part of staircase _____

5. not die/cruel _____

6. not later/opposite of lost (as in a race) _____

7. half of twenty/tennis court separation _____

8. pieces/a belt _____

9. flying mammals/knife injury _____

10. pull out from a dresser/prize _____

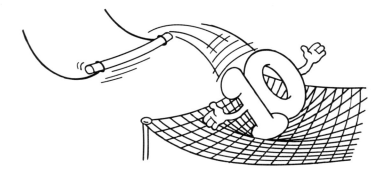

Graphing Favorites

Directions: Study the pie graph, and then answer the questions.

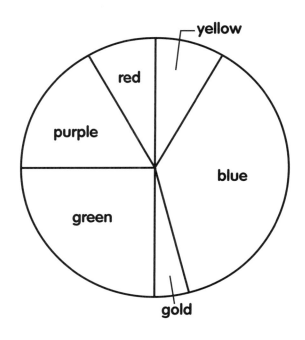

1. What was the most popular color?

   _____

2. What was the least popular color?

   _____

3. Which two colors had the same popularity?

   _____

4. Which color had twice the popularity of red?

   _____

5. Name three colors which make up half the

   graph. _____

Directions: Study the pie graph, and then answer the questions.

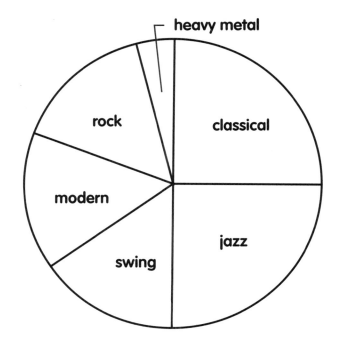

6. Which were the two most popular types of

   music?_____

7. Which was the least popular type of music?

   _____

8. What fraction of the total music selection

   was jazz? _____

9. Which two types of music make up half

   the total?_____

10. What is your favorite type of music?

    _____

Put Them Together

Directions: For each group of sentences below, write one sentence that includes all the necessary information. Add description (i.e., adjectives and adverbs) to strengthen the sentence even more. The first one has been done for you.

1. Grandpa read the newspaper.
   Grandpa drank his coffee.

   Grandpa read the Sunday newspaper
   while he drank his hot coffee.
   _____

2. The teachers went to the school assembly.
   The students went to the school assembly.

   _____
   _____
   _____

3. The girl likes picnics.
   The girl likes exploring.

   _____
   _____
   _____

4. The children visited the museum.
   It was a class field trip.

   _____
   _____
   _____

5. The kittens were playful.
   The kittens chased balls.
   The balls had bells in them.

   _____
   _____
   _____

6. Caroline chose a nice spot.
   It was near a brook.
   It was peaceful.

   _____
   _____
   _____

7. A crane came to the building.   _____

   The crane had a wrecking ball.   _____

   The crane knocked down the building. _____

   People watched it crumble.   _____

Dollars and Cents

Directions: Read each problem below. Write the coins and bills used to count back the change under the problem. The first one has been done for you.

1. The comic book cost $5.86. Tim gave the cashier $10.00. How much change did he receive?

    4 x $1.00
    1 x $ .10
  + 4 x $ .01
  ―――――――――
    $4.14

2. The bill for the Johnson family to get into the movies was $42.27. Mr. Johnson gave the cashier $50.00. How much change did he receive?

3. The total cost for the party supplies was $32.18. Aunt Jenny gave the cashier $35.00. How much change did she receive?

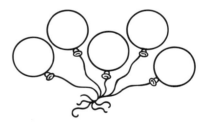

Directions: Rewrite each problem vertically and solve. Watch your signs.

4. $14.88 – $9.20

5. $490.01 + $24.51

6. $159.20 + $3.10

7. $84.39 – $62.94

Amphibians

Directions: Read the selection, and circle the correct answers.

What is an amphibian? An amphibian is an animal that spends part of its life underwater and part on land. When amphibians are underwater, they breathe with gills. When they are on land, they breathe with lungs. They are cold-blooded. This means that their body temperature changes depending on the temperature around them.

There are three different kinds of amphibians. The first group is newts and salamanders. These animals are about three inches long. They have four legs and four "**fingers**" on each leg. They are red-orange and transform to the color green.

The second type is frogs and toads. Frogs and toads are very similar. Toads have a warty back and spend less time in the water. They both eat insects and other small animals. Frogs begin as tadpoles. They spend time close to the water so that they can lay their eggs.

The last group is caecilians. These are wormlike creatures. Millions of years ago, there were other types of amphibians, but they are now extinct.

1. How is an amphibian different than most mammals?

   a. An amphibian eats different foods.

   b. An amphibian breathes underwater with gills.

   c. The amphibian is very territorial.

   d. An amphibian can swim.

2. Why is the word *fingers* in quotation marks in the passage?

   a. The author isn't sure it is the right word to use.

   b. The author is using it to show that they look and work like fingers.

   c. They don't become fingers until later.

   d. The author isn't sure of what to call these things.

3. What are the similarities between a frog and a toad?

   a. They both eat insects and other small animals.

   c. They are both wormlike creatures.

   b. They are both endangered species.

   d. They both begin as tadpoles.

4. What does the passage say about some amphibians millions of years ago?

   a. There is not enough information about them.

   b. There are new species being discovered every day.

   c. They are now extinct.

Time Change

Directions: Read each situation below, and write your answers on the lines.

1. Grandma is coming in exactly 2 days. In how many hours will Grandma be coming?

   _____ hours

2. Tom finished the race in 420 seconds. In how many minutes did he finish the race?

   _____ minutes

3. How many hours are there in 360 minutes?

   _____ hours

4. How many minutes are there in 2 hours and 18 minutes?

   _____ minutes

5. How many days are there in 96 hours?

   _____ days

6. How many seconds are there in 2 minutes and 45 seconds?

   _____ seconds

7. The movie marathon lasted for 72 hours. How many days did the marathon last?

   _____ days

Describe It

Directions: Adjectives are the describing words that add important details to the nouns in your writing. Underline all of the nouns in the following sentences. Revise the sentences to include one strong adjective before each noun.

1. The girl ran down the sidewalk._____

   _____

2. The frog hid under a mushroom._____

   _____

3. Dribbling down his chin was sauce. _____

   _____

4. A balloon floated into the sky. _____

   _____

5. The truck rumbled onto the road. _____

   _____

6. Fruit ripened in the basket._____

   _____

7. Frightened by the noise, the children cried. _____

   _____

8. The sun and wind dried the clothes. _____

   _____

9. The boys and girls laughed at the magician. _____

   _____

10. In the office, a nurse tended to the child. _____

   _____

Math Grab Bag

Week 8: Thursday

Directions: Solve the problems. Remember to work out the parentheses first.

1. 7 + (3 x 4) = _____

2. (6 x 5) + 7 = _____

3. (6 x 9) – 3 = _____

4. (8 x 2) + (3 x 4) = _____

5. (2 x 10) + (3 x 10) = _____

6. (5 x 2) + (6 x 2) = _____

7. (9 x 9) + 9 = _____

8. (8 x 3) + 5 = _____

9. (7 x 3) + 10 = _____

10. 10 + (3 x 3) = _____

11. (3 x 3) + 3 = _____

12. (6 x 7) + (6 x 7) = _____

Directions: Find the missing number facts.

13. 6 x _____ = 60

14. 7 x _____ = 49

15. _____ x 8 = 64

16. 10 x _____ = 70

17. 5 x _____ = 25

18. 9 x _____ = 81

19. 4 x _____ = 24

20. 7 x _____ = 14

21. 10 x _____ = 0

Directions: Fill in the spaces to complete the patterns.

22. 2, 4, 6, 8, _____ , 12

23. 6, 9, _____ , 15, 18, _____

24. 20, _____ , 40, 50, _____ , 70

25. 21, 28, _____ , _____ , 49, 56

26. 20, 25, _____ , _____ , _____

27. 16, 24, _____ , 40 , _____ , _____

Directions: Solve the problems.

28.   115
    x 4
    _____

29.   116
    x 7
    _____

30.   118
    x 8
    _____

31.   112
    x 8
    _____

32.   111
    x 3
    _____

Pros and Cons

Pros and cons are points for and against an idea that is being discussed. They are usually written in single sentences in order of importance.

Directions: Read the selection, and then answer the questions.

Should Children Always Wear Sunscreen?

> The topic is usually a question to be answered.

Pros (For)

> Positive points are in order of importance.

1. Children should wear sunscreen all the time because, without it, they can get skin cancer when they are older.

2. If children wear sunscreen continually, they won't get sunburned because sunscreen protects their skin.

3. If children wear sunscreen all the time, they will keep their natural skin color that they were born with.

> One point per number

Cons (Against)

> Negative points are in order of importance.

1. There's no point in wearing sunscreen when we're indoors or when it is raining.

2. People already wear hats to protect them from the sun, so they don't need to wear sunscreen, too.

3. Some people actually like to have suntanned skin, and sunscreen slows the tanning of their skin.

> Reasons make an argument believable.

1. Circle the correct answer. This discussion is about

   a. skin color.   b. sunburn.   c. wearing sunscreen.

2. Complete this sentence. The most serious effect of going without sunscreen protection is . . .

   _____

3. Do you know what *sunburn* is? If not, then look it up. Explain in one complete sentence.

   _____

4. Circle the correct answer. Hats protects us against sunburn by

   a. keeping our heads cool.

   b. keeping the sun's rays from our face and ears.

   c. keeping rain off our hair.

Top 10

Directions: Here's this week's top 10 Rock 'n' Roll chart. Next to each song is its movement since last week. For example, "Rock Around the Clock" has moved up seven places, so it must have been number 8 last week. Use the information to work out all of last week's chart.

Who was at the top of the charts? _____

This Week	Last Week
1. Rock Around the Clock (up 7)	1. #8
2. Shake, Rattle and Roll (up 8)	2.
3. That'll Be the Day (down 2)	3.
4. Peggy Sue (steady)	4.
5. Love Potion No. 9 (down 2)	5.
6. Wild One (up 3)	6.
7. Run Around Sue (down 2)	7.
8. Heartbreak Hotel (down 2)	8.
9. Shakin' All Over (down 2)	9.
10. Da Doo Ron Ron (down 8)	10.

Toothpicks

Directions: Use 12 "toothpicks" and follow the directions. Each box is a continuation of the previous box. Draw the diagrams you complete.

1. Start with 12 toothpicks in box 1.

2. In box 2, remove two toothpicks and make 2 squares.

3. In box 3, move two toothpicks and make 3 squares.

1.

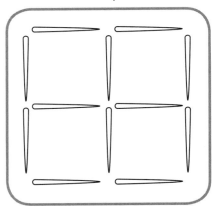

2.

3.

All About Me

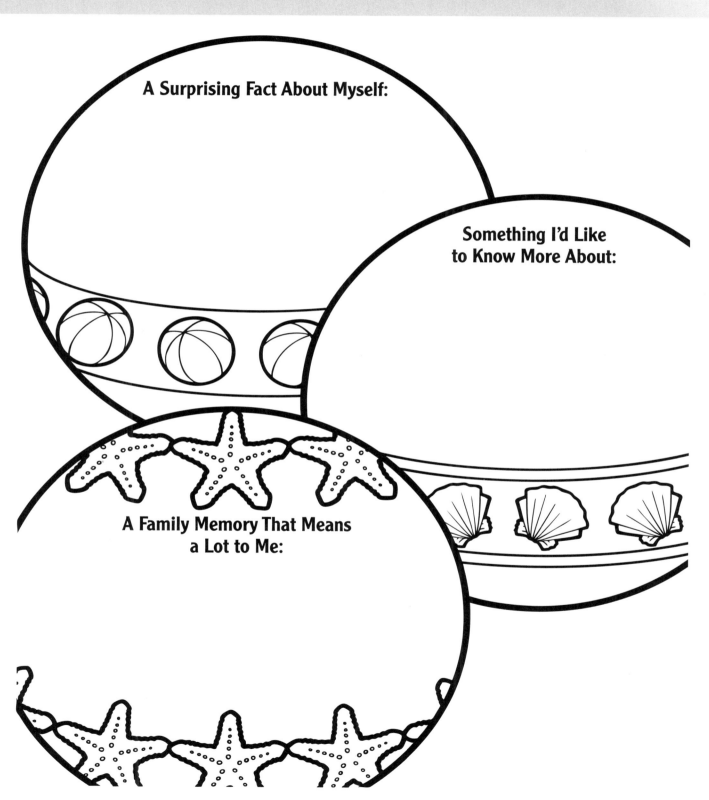

A Surprising Fact About Myself:

Something I'd Like
to Know More About:

A Family Memory That Means
a Lot to Me:

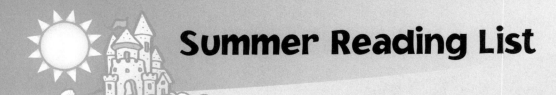

Summer Reading List

○ **Before We Were Free** by Julia Alvarez

Anita must hide with her family in the Dominican Republic during the 1960s. She is an average twelve-year-old child. She keeps a secret diary where she discusses her situation as well as her obsession with boys and her appearance.

Themes: family ties, courage, the cost of freedom

○ **The Secret School** by Avi

Ida Bidson is only fourteen years old when she takes over as teacher of a remote one-room schoolhouse after the regular teacher quits. Could Ida be the "secret" teacher of all the students for the rest of the year?

Themes: following a dream, secrecy, hope

○ **Jim Thorpe's Bright Path** by Joseph Bruchac

Jim Thorpe was the greatest Native American athlete. This book focuses on how his boyhood set the stage for his international fame.

Themes: importance of hard work, tenacity, competition

○ **Keeper of the Doves** by Betsy Byars

In Kentucky in the late 1880s, five sisters cannot understand why their father takes care of their scary neighbor.

Themes: family loyalty, kindness, empathy

○ **The Janitor's Boy** by Andrew Clements

Jack's father is a janitor at his school, and Jack's classmates ridicule him for it.

Themes: family loyalty, important truths, standing up to ridicule

○ **Granny Torrelli Makes Soup** by Sharon Creech

A long-term friendship is strained when a new girl moves into the neighborhood.

Themes: family love, friendship, Italian cooking

○ **Gandhi** by Demi

Gandhi's life and work is told in a language easily grasped by elementary students. Beautifully illustrated.

Themes: humanity, humility, empathy

○ **The Several Lives of Orphan Jack** by Sarah Ellis

Jack is an optimistic orphan who decides that the school for orphans is not the best for his outlook on life. He sets off on his own to find his fortune and see the world.

Themes: self-reliance, strength of character, optimism

Making the Most of Summertime Reading

When reading these books with your child, you may wish to ask the questions below. The sharing of questions and answers will enhance and improve your child's reading comprehension skills.

○ Why did you choose this book to read?

○ Name a character from the story that you like. Why do you like him or her?

○ Where does the story take place? Do you want to vacation there?

○ Name a problem that occurs in the story. How is it resolved?

○ What is the best part of the story so far? Describe it!

○ What do you think is going to happen next in the story? Make a prediction!

○ Who are the important characters in the story? Why are they important?

○ What is the book about?

○ What are two things you have learned by reading this book?

○ Would you tell your friend to read this book? Why or why not?

Summer Reading List

☼ **Boxes for Katje** by Candace Fleming

In postwar Holland, a Dutch girl receives a care package from an Indiana girl. This act soon becomes a community effort.

Themes: gratitude, humanity, kindness

☼ **The Million Dollar Shot** by Dan Gutman

Eleven-year-old Eddie lives in a Louisiana trailer park with his widowed mother. A stroke of luck gives him a chance to win a million dollars by sinking a foul shot at the National Basketball Association finals.

Themes: poverty, life values, future dreams

☼ **Babymouse #8: Puppy Love** by Jennifer L. Holm and Matthew Holm

In this graphic novel, Babymouse has had her challenges with pets, but she feels confident that getting a dog will be a different experience. Will Babymouse end up getting the animal of her dreams?

Themes: love for animals, determination, humor

☼ **Under the Quilt of Night** by Deborah Hopkinson

A young slave uses the Underground Railroad to make her escape to the North. Beautifully illustrated.

Themes: courage, hope, friendship

☼ **Any Small Goodness: A Novel of the Barrio** by Tony Johnston

Short vignettes (chapters) make this a good choice for reading aloud. Arturo and his family leave Mexico for East Los Angeles.

Themes: family relationships, cultural differences, coping with difficulties

☼ **Sweet Potato Pie** by Kathleen D. Lindsey

An African American family in the early 1900s discovers a delicious way to save the family farm. Includes a sweet potato pie recipe.

Themes: close family relationships, working together to achieve a goal, ethnic cooking

☼ **A Corner of the Universe** by Ann M. Martin

Hattie's world is turned upside down with the arrival of a mentally challenged uncle. Set in the 1960s, it draws on the novelist's life.

Themes: difficult family responsibilities, making the best of a difficult situation

☼ **Love to Mama: A Tribute to Mothers** by Pat Mora (editor)

Thirteen Latin American poets present their collection of works, combining English and Spanish, which describe relationships between mothers, grandmothers, and children.

Themes: multigenerational relationships, Latino culture, family love

☼ **The Girl with 500 Middle Names** by Margaret Peterson Haddix

Janie realizes that everyone around her has more money than her family, who recently moved to the suburbs so she could go to a better school.

Themes: life values, pride, family relationships

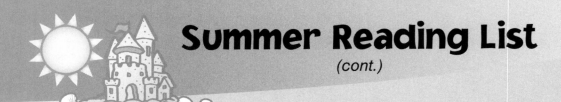

Summer Reading List
(cont.)

☼ **The Hickory Chair** by Lisa Rowe Fraustino

A blind boy's grandmother dies but leaves him an important gift that impacts his life.

Themes: multigenerational relationships, grief, passing on of family beliefs

☼ **Dog-of-the-Sea-Waves** by James Rumford

In English and Hawaiian, this novel is about the first humans who set foot on the Hawaiian Islands. Manu and his four brothers must deal with this new land and then return home for their families.

Themes: man vs. nature, exploration

☼ **19 Varieties of Gazelle: Poems of the Middle East** by Naomi Shihab Nye

Sixty poems about the Middle East are showcased in response to the tragic events of September 11, 2001. These are told through the eyes of both Americans and Palestinians.

Themes: hope, conflict, war, relationships

☼ **Maniac Magee** by Jerry Spinelli

This Newbery Award book chronicles a resourceful orphan who must make his own way in the world after running away from an impossible living situation.

Themes: race relationships, making the best of bad situations, hope

☼ **The Kite Fighters** by Linda Sue Park

It is 1473 in Korea, and an eleven-year-old boy and his older brother must deal with a rivalry when the older boy receives special treatment from his father as both compete in a New Year kite competition.

Themes: sibling rivalry, favoritism, family relationships

☼ **The Boy Who Could Fly Without a Motor** by Theodore Taylor

It's 1935 and Jon Jeffers is stuck on an island off the coast of San Francisco with only his mother and lighthouse-keeper father. An ancient magician arrives and offers the boy the secret of human flight.

Themes: friendship, fantasy, family values

☼ **Dr. Frankenstein's Human Body Book** by Richard Walker

Each reader of this book becomes Dr. Frankenstein's assistant as he creates a human being. Photos and illustrations demonstrate how the human body works.

Themes: informative, technology

☼ **Tadpole** by Ruth White

Tad needs a home away from his abusive uncle. Even though his cousins are destitute, they welcome him into their home.

Themes: family love, abusive adults, gratitude

☼ **Millicent Min, Girl Genius** by Lisa Yee

An eleven-year-old Chinese American girl records the highs and lows of the summer before her senior year in high school.

Themes: cross-cultural respect, friendship, humor

Fun Ways to Love Books

Here are some fun ways that your child can expand on his or her reading. Most of these ideas will involve both you and your child; however, the wording has been directed towards your child because we want him or her to be inspired to love books.

Reading Survey

Conduct a survey to find out which books the people in your community loved as children. Include coaches, grocery-store cashiers, babysitters, and other adults you know. Share your findings with friends in order to create an even larger list so that you will always have good book recommendations!

Write to the Author

Many authors love to hear from their readers, especially when they hear what people liked best about their books. You can write to an author and send your letter in care of the book's publisher. The publisher's address is listed directly after the title page. Or you may go to the author's Web site and follow the directions for how to send the author a letter. (To make sure your author is still living, do a search on the Internet, typing the author's name into a search engine.)

A Comic Book

Turn your favorite book into a comic book. Fold at least two sheets of paper in half, and staple them so they make a book. With a ruler and pencil, draw boxes across each page to look like blank comic strips. Then, draw the story of your book as if it were a comic. Draw pictures of your characters, and have words coming out of their mouths—just as in a real comic strip.

Write a Sequel

What happens to the characters in your book after you finish reading the final page? Why not create a sequel? A sequel is a book that is published after the first book has enjoyed success among readers. Sequels generally pick up where the first book left off. For example, the sequel to Madeleine L'Engle's novel *A Wrinkle in Time* is *A Wind in the Door.*

Learn a New Skill

What skills are mentioned in your favorite book? Perhaps a character learns to ride a unicycle. Other characters may create beautiful pottery, train dogs, take black-and-white photographs, or bake five-layer cakes. Identify a skill mentioned in your book. Gather together the materials you'll need to learn this skill. Keep in mind that learning a new skill may take several weeks or months. Commit to practicing this skill at least twice a week. Keep a journal detailing your growing abilities.

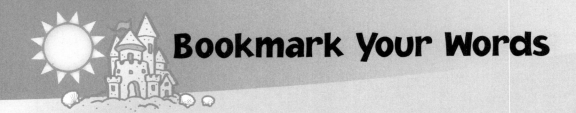

Bookmark Your Words

Make summertime reading lots of fun with these reading log glasses. Have your child fill in the glasses after his or her daily reading. Once your child has completed the glasses, he or she can cut them out and use them as bookmarks.

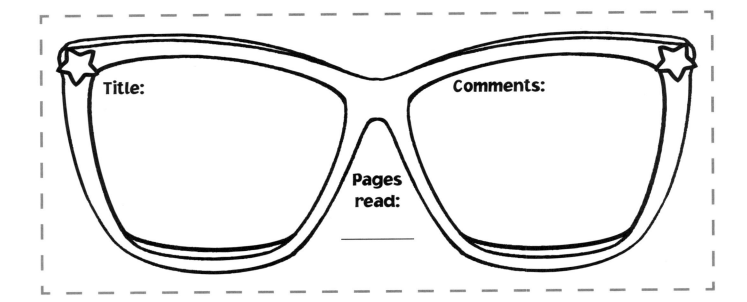

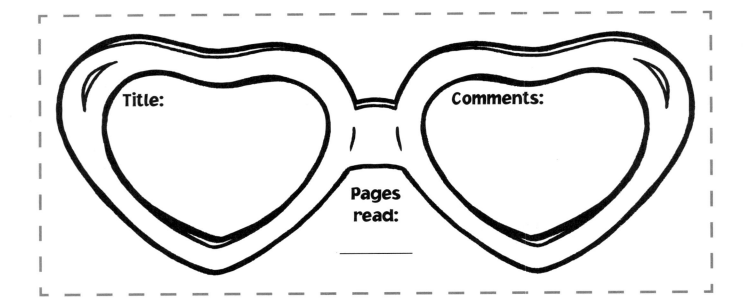

This page may be reproduced as many times as needed.

Read-Together Chart

Does your father read books to you before bed? Perhaps your mother reads to the family at breakfast? Your grandparents may enjoy reading books to you after school or on the weekends. You and your family members can create a Read-Together Chart and fill it in to keep track of all the books you've read together.

Here are two Read-Together Charts. The first one is a sample. The second one has been left blank, so you can add your own categories and books.

Sample Chart

Book We Read	Who Read It?	Summary	Our Review
The Secret Garden	My older sister read it to me.	It's about a spoiled girl who learns to love nature and people.	We like this book. The characters are funny, and the illustrations are beautiful!

Your Chart

This page may be reproduced as many times as needed.

Journal Topics

Choose one of these journal topics each day. Make sure you add enough detail so someone else reading this will clearly be able to know at least four of the following:

❍ **who**   ❍ **what**   ❍ **when**   ❍ **where**   ❍ **why**   ❍ **how**

1. I always get upset when . . .
2. If I could create another holiday to celebrate, it would be . . .
3. If I could design my own school, it would look like . . .
4. One time, when spending a night away from home, I . . .
5. One of my talents is . . .
6. If my favorite book was made into a movie, the most important part that I would want to be included is . . .
7. One of my favorite trips was . . .
8. One of my funniest experiences was when I . . .
9. I always forget to . . .
10. I like to hang out at the mall because . . . *or* I do not like to hang out at the mall because . . .
11. A really good teacher always . . .
12. I agree that smoking should be banned from public places because . . .
13. If I won an award, it would be for . . .
14. If I could plan a perfect day for my friend and myself, we would . . .
15. On weekends, I like to . . .
16. Since graffiti is such a problem, I think people who are caught should . . .
17. If I could create a new invention to help fourth graders like myself, I would . . .
18. One time, when I had to talk in front of a large group, I . . .
19. Whenever I want to relax, the music I want to listen to is . . .
20. My last argument was about . . .
21. If children get an allowance, their household chores should be . . .
22. One habit I would really like to break is . . .
23. My favorite relative is _____ because . . .
24. I think the amount of junk food a young person should be allowed to eat is . . .
25. One great advertisement (commercial) that I've seen recently is . . .

Learning Experiences

Here are some fun, low-cost activities that you can do with your child. You'll soon discover that these activities can be stimulating, educational, and complementary to the other exercises in this book.

Flash Cards

Make up all types of flash cards. Depending on your child's interest and grade level, these cards might feature enrichment words, math problems, or states and capitals. You can create them yourself with markers or on a computer. Let your child help cut pictures out of magazines and glue them on. Then, find a spot outdoors, and go through the flash cards with your child.

Project Pantry

Find a spot in your house where you can store supplies. This might be a closet or a bin that stays in one spot. Get some clean paint cans or buckets. Fill them with all types of craft and art supplies. Besides the typical paints, markers, paper, scissors, and glue, include some more unusual things, such as tiles, artificial flowers, and wrapping paper. This way, whenever you and your child want to do a craft project, you have everything you need at that moment.

The Local Library

Check out everything that your local library has to offer. Most libraries offer summer reading programs with various incentives. Spend an afternoon choosing and then reading books together.

How Much Does It Cost?

If you go out for a meal, have your child help total the bill. Write down the cost of each person's meal. Then, have your child add them all together. You can vary this and make it much simpler by having your child just figure out the cost of an entrée and a drink or the cost of three desserts. You might want to round the figures first.

Nature Scavenger Hunt

Take a walk, go to a park, or hike in the mountains. But before you go, create a scavenger hunt list for your child. This can consist of all sorts of things found in nature. Make sure your child has a bag to carry everything he or she finds. (Be sure to check ahead of time about the rules or laws regarding removing anything.) You might include things like a leaf with pointed edges, a speckled rock, and a twig with two small limbs on it. Take a few minutes to look at all the things your child has collected, and check them off the list.

Take a Trip, and Keep a Journal

If you are going away during the summer, have your child keep a journal. Depending on his or her age, this can take a different look. A young child can collect postcards and paste them into a blank journal. He or she can also draw pictures of places he or she is visiting. An older child can keep a traditional journal and draw pictures. Your child can also do a photo-journal if a camera is available for him or her to use.

Web Sites

Math Web Sites

☼ **AAA Math:** http://www.aaamath.com
This site contains hundreds of pages of basic math skills divided by grade or topic.

☼ **AllMath.com:** http://www.allmath.com
This site has math flashcards, biographies of mathematicians, and a math glossary.

☼ **BrainBashers:** http://www.brainbashers.com
This is a unique collection of brainteasers, games, and optical illusions.

☼ **Coolmath.com:** http://www.coolmath.com
Explore this amusement park of mathematics! Have fun with the interactive activities.

☼ **Mrs. Glosser's Math Goodies:** http://www.mathgoodies.com
This is a free educational Web site featuring interactive worksheets, puzzles, and more!

Reading and Writing Web Sites

☼ **Aesop's Fables:** http://www.umass.edu/aesop
This site has almost forty of the fables. Both traditional and modern versions are presented.

☼ **American Library Association:** http://ala.org
Visit this site to find out both the past and present John Newbery Medal and Randolph Caldecott Medal winners.

☼ **Book Adventure:** http://www.bookadventure.com
This site features a free reading incentive program dedicated to encouraging children in grades K–8 to read.

☼ **Chateau Meddybemps—Young Writers Workshop:** http://www.meddybemps.com/9.700.html
Use the provided story starters to help your child write a story.

☼ **Fairy Godmother:** http://www.fairygodmother.com
This site will capture your child's imagination and spur it on to wonderful creativity.

☼ **Grammar Gorillas:** http://www.funbrain.com/grammar
Play grammar games on this site that proves that grammar can be fun!

☼ **Graphic Organizers:** http://www.eduplace.com/graphicorganizer
Use these graphic organizers to help your child write in an organized manner.

☼ **Rhymezone:** http://www.rhymezone.com
Type in the word you want to rhyme. If there is a rhyming word to match your word, you'll find it here.

☼ **Storybook:** http://www.kids-space.org/story/story.html
Storybook takes children's stories and publishes them on this Web site. Just like in a library, children can choose a shelf and read stories.

Web Sites *(cont.)*

Reading and Writing Web Sites *(cont.)*

☼ **Wacky Web Tales:** http://www.eduplace.com/tales/index.html
This is a great place for budding writers to submit their stories and read other children's writing.

☼ **Write on Reader:** http://library.thinkquest.org/J001156
Children can visit Write on Reader to gain a love of reading and writing.

General Web Sites

☼ **Animal Photos:** http://nationalzoo.si.edu
This site offers wonderful pictures of animals, as well as virtual zoo visits.

☼ **Animal Planet:** http://animal.discovery.com
Best for older kids, children can watch videos or play games at this site for animal lovers.

☼ **Congress for Kids:** http://www.congressforkids.net
Children can go to this site to learn all about the branches of the United States government.

☼ **Dinosaur Guide:** http://dsc.discovery.com/dinosaurs
This is an interactive site on dinosaurs that goes beyond just learning about the creatures.

☼ **The Dinosauria:** http://www.ucmp.berkeley.edu/diapsids/dinosaur.html
This site focuses on dispelling dinosaur myths. Read about fossils, history, and more.

☼ **Earthquake Legends:** http://www.fema.gov/kids/eqlegnd.htm
On this site, children can read some of the tales behind earthquakes that people of various cultures once believed.

☼ **The Electronic Zoo:** http://netvet.wustl.edu/e-zoo.htm
This site has links to thousands of animal sites covering every creature under the sun!

☼ **Great Buildings Online:** http://www.greatbuildings.com
This gateway to architecture around the world and across history documents a thousand buildings and hundreds of leading architects.

☼ **Maggie's Earth Adventures:** http://www.missmaggie.org
Join Maggie and her dog, Dude, on a wonderful Earth adventure.

☼ **Mr. Dowling's Electronic Passport:** http://www.mrdowling.com/index.html
This is an incredible history and geography site.

☼ **Tropical Twisters:** http://kids.mtpe.hq.nasa.gov/archive/hurricane/index.html
Take an in-depth look at hurricanes, from how they're created to how dangerous they are.

Handwriting Chart

Aa   *Bb*   *Cc*   *Dd*

Ee   *Ff*   *Gg*   *Hh*

Ii   *Jj*   *Kk*   *Ll*

Mm   *Nn*   *Oo*   *Pp*

Qq   *Rr*   *Ss*   *Tt*

Uu   *Vv*   *Ww*

Xx   *Yy*   *Zz*

Proofreading Marks

Editor's Mark	Meaning	Example
≡	capitalize	they fished in lake tahoe.
/	make it lowercase	Five $tudents missed the $us.
sp.	spelling mistake	The day was clowdy and cold.
⊙	add a period	Tomorrow is a holiday⊙
ℓ	delete (remove)	One person knew the the answer.
∧	add a word	Six pups were in the litter.
⟨,⟩	add a comma	He planted peas, corn, and squash.
∿	reverse words or letters	An otter swam in the bed kelp.
⌄	add an apostrophe	The child's bike was blue.
⌄ ⌄	add quotation marks	Why can't I go? she cried.
#	make a space	He ate two red apples.
‿	close the space	Her favorite game is soft ball.
¶	begin a new paragraph	to know. Next on the list

Multiplication Chart

X	0	1	2	3	4	5	6	7	8	9	10	11	12
0	0	0	0	0	0	0	0	0	0	0	0	0	0
1	0	1	2	3	4	5	6	7	8	9	10	11	12
2	0	2	4	6	8	10	12	14	16	18	20	22	24
3	0	3	6	9	12	15	18	21	24	27	30	33	36
4	0	4	8	12	16	20	24	28	32	36	40	44	48
5	0	5	10	15	20	25	30	35	40	45	50	55	60
6	0	6	12	18	24	30	36	42	48	54	60	66	72
7	0	7	14	21	28	35	42	49	56	63	70	77	84
8	0	8	16	24	32	40	48	56	64	72	80	88	96
9	0	9	18	27	36	45	54	63	72	81	90	99	108
10	0	10	20	30	40	50	60	70	80	90	100	110	120
11	0	11	22	33	44	55	66	77	88	99	110	121	132
12	0	12	24	36	48	60	72	84	96	108	120	132	144

Measurement Tools

Measurement Conversion Chart

 cups (c.)	1	2	4	8	16
pints (pt.)	$\frac{1}{2}$	1	2	4	8
quarts (qt.)	$\frac{1}{4}$	$\frac{1}{2}$	1	2	4
gallons (gal.)	$\frac{1}{16}$	$\frac{1}{8}$	$\frac{1}{4}$	$\frac{1}{2}$	1

Inch Ruler Cutout

Directions: Cut out the two ruler parts, and tape them together.

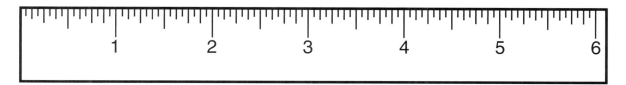

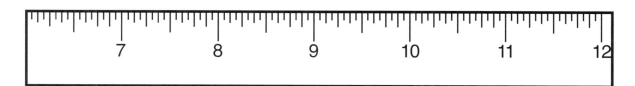

Centimeter Ruler Cutout

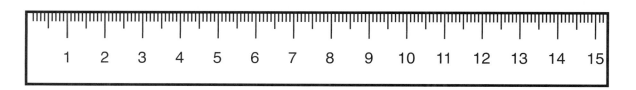

This page may be reproduced as many times as needed.

Answer Key

Page 11
1. 15,481
2. 226
3. 2,785
4. 8,494
5. 1,495
6. 16,218

Page 12
1. e
2. a
3. b
4. c
5. d
6. helm
7. drowsy
8. conform
9. essential
10. surroundings

Page 13
1. 90°
2. 180°
3. 360°
4. 360°
5. 180°
6. 270°
7. 270°
8. 360°
9. 180°
10. 90°
11. 180°
12. 90°

Page 14
Answers will vary.

Page 15

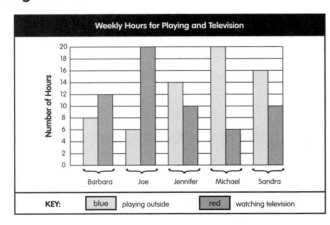

Page 16
Answers will vary; possible answers:
- *Main Idea*: Tiger was a funny cat.
- *Supporting Detail*: He drank from the aquarium.
- *Supporting Detail*: He would lap up the water when they gave the dog a bath.

Page 17
1. $\frac{4}{7}$
2. $\frac{1}{6}$
3. $\frac{3}{10}$
4. $\frac{3}{8}$
5. $\frac{1}{3}$
6. $\frac{5}{12}$

Page 18
Answers will vary.

Page 19
1. pay
2. hold
3. move
4. make
5. enjoy
6. bring
7. want
8. keep

Page 20
1. beach
2. goggles
3. swim
4. sink
5. wave
6. pool
7. sand
8. dive
9. race *or* pace
10. kick
11. flip *or* drip
12. water
13. flipper
14. float
15. laps *or* caps

Page 21
1. c
2. b
3. 60 stuffed bears
4. 37 birds

Page 22
1. present
2. future
3. past
4. present
5. past
6. Maria always **wore** a T-shirt over her bathing suit in the pool.
7. We **pitched** a tent for shade when we **went** on a picnic.
8. The day **was** hot and bright, so we **wore** hats and sunscreen.

Page 23
1. 24 sides
2. c
3. 50°F
4. 28 ft.

Page 24
1. a
2. b
3. b

Page 25
1. 6
2. 12
3. 6
4. 8
5. 9
6. 12
7. 5
8. 12
9. 6
10. 9
11. 7
12. 11
13. 6
14. 9
15. 9
16. 11
17. 7
18. 7
19. 6
20. 6
21. 9
22. 4
23. 11
24. 4

Page 26
Answers will vary.

Page 27
1. $49 + $57 = $106
2. $32 + $57 = $89
3. $26 + $32 = $58
4. $64 + $17 + $49 = $130

Answer Key (cont.)

Page 27 (cont.)

5. $17 + $64 = $81
6. $26 + $57 + $32 = $115

Page 28

1. 4   3. 3   5. 2
2. 1   4. 6   6. 5

Page 29

There are many ways to travel. People can travel by plane, boat, or train. Cars and buses are other ways to travel. Bicycles, tricycles, scooters, and skateboards are good for getting around. A fun way to travel is on a horse or a donkey. Some people can even travel in a spaceship!

Page 30

1. 276   4. 954
2. 61   5. 977
3. 810

Page 31

1. 100 books   5. 50 cones
2. mystery   6. strawberry
3. 30 more students 7. 20 more cones
4. joke; mystery   8. 180 cones

Page 32

Answers will vary; possible answers:

1. Daryl and his family are moving to a colder climate.
2. Dishes have been wrapped in newspaper.
   Larry said, "It might be some time before I see you again."
   Larry said, "No more beach clothes for you!"

Page 33

1. $8.19   6. $6.74
2. $70.34   7. $17.87
3. $5.08   8. $5.09
4. $31.89   9. $5.73
5. $57.14   10. $11.94

Page 34

1. The school
2. The dog
3. The sun
4. Fourth graders
5. Spring

Remaining answers will vary.

Page 35

1. b
2. 36 candy bars
3. $1,575
4. 192 cans

Page 36

1. b   2. b   3. c

Page 37

1. A   2. b   3. b

Page 38

2. Everyone was laughing.
3. Erika has a cold.
4. The cat jumped off the log.
5. They ate the birthday cake.
6. She can do a backward flip.
7. Summer is the time for fishing.

Remaining answers will vary.

Page 39

Triangles = 27
Quadrilaterals = 40

Page 40

Answers will vary; possible answers:

1. fin, find, foil, fond, fold, fob
2. left, lent, lend, lam, lit, lid, lad, life, lie, lime, let, lint, leaf, lean, lame, led, lane, late, land, lain, laid, lead, lift, line, lied, lifted, lined, lite
3. call, carts, calls, car, cart, cars, cast, cabs, cab, crab, crabs, cat, cats, crib, cribs

Page 41

3. 73 R1   7. 72 R5   10. 45 R3
4. 132 R3   8. 29 R7   11. 104 R1
5. 123 R2   9. 214 R1   12. 89 R6
6. 96 R1

Page 42

Answers will vary.

Page 43

1. c
2. 30 18   21
    6   6   15
   15   3   45
3. Top to bottom: orange, yellow, green, white

Answer Key (cont.)

Page 44

Answers will vary; possible answers:

1. Julia would tell about the sites in Belize. She didn't give any details about the sites in her letter.

2. Making predictions helps keep readers interested because they want to keep reading to see if they are right.

Page 45

1. 90	3. 80	5. 29
2. 70	4. 24	6. 89

Page 46

Answers will vary.

Page 47

1. 40	6. 900
2. 80	7. 700
3. 60	8. 700
4. 190	9. 53 items
5. 5,300	10. 7 years old

Page 48

1. a	5. d	8. A
2. e	6. S	9. S
3. b	7. A	10. A
4. c		

Page 49

Answers will vary; possible answers:

3. A *calot* is a figure that is divided symmetrically in half using a vertical line.

6. A *wiggle* is a circular figure. Notice each shape is always rounded on the outer edge.

Page 50

Anne—volleyball

Elise—basketball

Ethan—swimming

Katie—baseball

Kevin—track

Logan—soccer

Page 51

1. d	6. c
2. c	7. b
3. a	8. d
4. b	9. 600 inches
5. a	10. 1,198,229 people

Page 52

Answers will vary; possible answers:

Clues:

☼ entered her office

☼ grabbed her notebook and pen

☼ said, "Now, that's news!"

☼ asked the caller a series of questions

☼ said, "This'll be great for the front page!"

Inferences:

Lena is a newspaper reporter since she needs to know answers, and she says that "This'll be great for the front page!"

Page 53

1–9. All answers are ÷ and =.

10. $42 \div 6 = 7$	21. 3 R1
11. $9 \div 3 = 3$	22. 2 R1
12. $21 \div 7 = 3$	23. 4 R2
13. $36 \div 6 = 6$	24. 2 R1
14. $10 \div 2 = 5$	25. 2 R1
15. $28 \div 4 = 7$	26. 1 R7
16. $45 \div 5 = 9$	27. 4 R3
17. $6 \div 6 = 1$	28. 8 R2
18. $32 \div 8 = 4$	29. 2 R8
19. 4 R4	30. 7 R1
20. 1 R2	

Page 54

1. When I went to the store, I saw my teacher, Mrs. Roe.

2. My family will go to Disneyland in July.

3. I am reading <u>Old Yeller</u> this week.

4. My sister Sarah says her favorite subject is Spanish.

5. On Wednesday, we will celebrate Groundhog Day.

6. My brother said that Mom was a cheerleader at Eastside High School.

7. In August, we're going to visit Aunt Mary in San Francisco, California.

8. Benji had a birthday, so she sang "Happy Birthday to You."

9. My friend Rosa speaks Spanish, and I speak English.

10. My neighbor Julia is going to Paris, France, next June.

Answer Key *(cont.)*

Page 55

Estimates will vary for answers 1–8.

1. 1 hr. 45 min.
2. 1 hr. 2 min.
3. 1 hr. 5 min.
4. 2 hr. 51 min.
5. 3 hr. 7 min.
6. 2 hr. 40 min.
7. 3 hr. 38 min.
8. 4 hr. 20 min.

Remaining answers will vary.

Page 56

Answers will vary; underlined sentences:

1. Today, however, her father was in an especially happy mood and agreed that she could use his car for the afternoon.
2. She rolled down the window and turned up the radio.
3. Jessica swerved to miss the dog and ended up running into the neighbors' trash cans.

Page 57

1. 0.6
2. 0.4
3. 0.09
4. 48.07
5. 2.7
6. 9.3
7. $\frac{7}{10}$
8. $\frac{2}{10}$
9. 2 slices
10. $6.25

Page 58

Answers will vary.

Page 59

1. leg swing
2. back flip(s)
3. pike
4. tuck
5. still rings
6. pommel horse
7. parallel bars
8. six man team

Page 60

Page 61

1. 624 feet
2. 325 feet
3. 358 feet
4. 195 feet
5. 4,875 feet; 405 feet
6. 61.54 meters
7. 6.15 meters
8. 23.08 meters

Page 62

1. <u>Chato and the Party Animals</u>
2. "Years Later"
3. <u>Glee</u>
4. "Dogs Are Man's Best Friend"
5. <u>Wicked</u>
6. <u>20,000 Leagues Under the Sea</u>
7. <u>Up</u>
8. <u>The Wizard of Oz</u>
9. "The Road Not Taken"
10. <u>The Indian in the Cupboard</u>

Page 63

1. 500 + 60 + 1
2. 9,000 + 10 + 1
3. 3,000 + 500 + 80 + 7
4. 4,000 + 400 + 4
5. 800 + 20 + 6
6. 8,000 + 900 + 90
8. 590 = five hundreds, eight tens, ten ones
9. 1,028 = (1 x 1,000) + (2 x 10) + (8 x 1)
10. 84 = seven tens, fourteen ones
11. 600 = six one-hundreds
12. 2,300 = no ones, no tens, three hundreds, two thousands
13. 875 = 800 + 70 + 5
14. 9,437 = seven ones, three tens, four hundreds, nine thousands
15. 1,902 = nineteen hundreds, two ones
16. 1,316
17. 649
18. 4,406
19. 2,003
20. 846
21. 9,041
22. 7,095
23. 1,723
24. 1,164
25. 5,000

Answer Key *(cont.)*

Page 64

2. ate away; b

3. huddled; a

4. hop, skip, and jump; a

5. yawn; c

6. grabbed; b

7. sleepy; a

Page 65

1. 20
2. 40
3. 80
4. 20
5. 60
6. 20
7. 40
8. 60
9. 40
10. 10
11. 80
12. 40
13. 200
14. 300
15. 400
16. 100
17. 500
18. 700
19. 300
20. 700
21. 900
22. 300
23. 800
24. 900
25. 3,000
26. 6,000
27. 7,000
28. 5,000
29. 2,000
30. 9,000
31. 2,000
32. 8,000
33. 6,000
34. 7,000
35. 6,000
36. 8,000

Page 66

Answers will vary.

Page 67

Missing parts are as follows:

1. 3, 16, 19, 16, 19, 3, 19, 16

2. 40, 35, 40, 16, 40, 16, 35, 40, 16

3. 2, 1, 2, 2, 2, 2, 1, 2

4. 7, 8, 6, 8, 7, 8, 6, 8, 6

5. 19, 29, 9, 19, 39, 19, 29, 39

6. circle, rectangle, triangle, circle, circle, rectangle, triangle, rectangle

7. arrow up, arrow left, arrow right, arrow left, arrow right, arrow up, arrow right, arrow up

8. heart, square, circle, square, heart, heart, square

9. circle, circle, circle, circle, circle, triangle, circle, circle, triangle

10. horizontal rectangle, vertical rectangle, horizontal rectangle, vertical rectangle, horizontal rectangle, horizontal rectangle, vertical rectangle, vertical rectangle, horizontal rectangle

11. 3, 6, 9, 18, 24, 33

12. 2, 4, 6, 14, 18, 24

Page 68

1. d   2. a   3. d   4. c

Page 69

1. Andre—letter, aunt, no stamp

2. Ben—bill, baker, Capitol building stamp

3. Cindy—postcard, mom, Mount Rushmore stamp

4. Daphne—package, dad, penguin stamp

Page 70

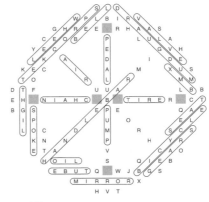

Page 71

1. f, 17
2. h, 56
3. a, 7
4. e, 8
5. d, 13
6. 10
7. 4
8. 6
9. 35
10. 69

Page 72

1. It meant that she needed to do her fair share of the work.

2. b

3. c

Page 73

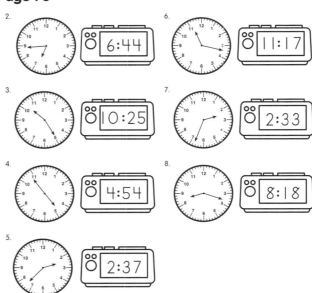

Answer Key (cont.)

Page 74

1. how many
2. what kind
3. how many
4. what kind
5. what kind
6. what kind
7. what kind
8. what kind
9. how many
10. what kind
11. how many
12. how many
13. what kind
14. how many
15. how many
16. what kind
17. how many
18. what kind
19. young, old
20. only, pair
21. good, guide
22. experienced, bird, powerful
23. <u>quiet</u>, <u>wooded</u>
24. <u>several</u>, <u>curious</u>
25. <u>different</u>, <u>small</u>

Page 75

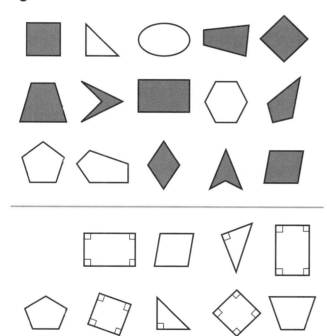

Page 76

1. c
2. In the packet of grass seeds, there must have also been weed seeds.
3. The cat ate him because he was too fat to run away.
4. She was so thin that she slipped down her straw into the lemonade.

Page 77

1. $2
2. $6
3. $3 \frac{1}{2}$ lbs.
4. $\frac{1}{2}$ lb.
5. $2 \frac{1}{2}$ lbs.
6. Saturday and Sunday
7. Monday
8. Sunday
9. 460 DVDs

Page 78

Answers will vary; possible answers:

1. wake
2. wash
3. dress
4. eat
5. brush teeth
6. The dog chased Jenny's cat.
7. The cat raced up the tree.
8. The cat wouldn't come down.
9. Jenny climbed the tree.
10. The cat climbed higher.
11. Jenny climbed higher.
12. Both were too frightened to climb down.

Remaining answers will vary.

Page 79

1. □
2. △
3. ○
4. ♡
5. ○
6. □
7. D
8. △
9. ♡
10. ▭

Page 80

1. tar/rat
2. raw/war
3. pot/top
4. pets/step
5. live/evil
6. now/won
7. ten/net
8. parts/strap
9. bats/stab
10. drawer/reward

Answer Key (cont.)

Page 81
1. blue
2. gold
3. red and yellow
4. purple
5. red, purple, green *or* yellow, blue, gold
6. classical and jazz
7. heavy metal
8. $\frac{1}{4}$
9. classical and jazz
10. Answers will vary.

Page 82
Answers will vary.

Page 83
2.
```
    1 x $ 5. 0 0
    2 x $ 1. 0 0
    2 x $ 0. 2 5
    2 x $ 0. 1 0
  + 3 x $ 0. 0 1
        $ 7. 7 3
```

3.
```
    2 x $ 1. 0 0
    3 x $ 0. 2 5
    1 x $ 0. 0 5
  + 2 x $ 0. 0 1
        $ 2. 8 2
```

4. $5.68
5. $514.52
6. $162.30
7. $21.45

Page 84
1. b   2. b   3. a   4. c

Page 85
1. 48 hours   5. 4 days
2. 7 minutes   6. 165 seconds
3. 6 hours   7. 3 days
4. 138 minutes

Page 86
Sentences will vary; nouns in sentences:
1. girl, sidewalk
2. frog, mushroom
3. chin, sauce
4. balloon, sky
5. truck, road
6. fruit, basket
7. noise, children
8. sun, wind, clothes
9. boys, girls, magician
10. office, nurse, child

Page 87

1. 19	12. 84	23. 12, 21
2. 37	13. 10	24. 30, 60
3. 51	14. 7	25. 35, 42
4. 28	15. 8	26. 30, 35, 40
5. 50	16. 7	27. 32, 48, 56
6. 22	17. 5	28. 460
7. 90	18. 9	29. 812
8. 29	19. 6	30. 944
9. 31	20. 2	31. 896
10. 19	21. 0	32. 333
11. 12	22. 10	

Page 88
1. c
2. the higher risk of getting skin cancer.
3. The UV rays of the sun burn the skin until it turns red and blisters.
4. b

Page 89
1. That'll Be the Day
2. Da Doo Ron Ron
3. Love Potion No. 9
4. Peggy Sue
5. Run Around Sue
6. Heartbreak Hotel
7. Shakin' All Over
8. Rock Around the Clock
9. Wild One
10. Shake, Rattle and Roll
"That'll Be the Day" was at the top.

Page 90
2.   3.